Decades of American History

AMERICA IN THE 1950s

CHARLES A. WILLS

Facts On File, Inc.

A Stonesong Press Book
Decades of American History: *America in the 1950s*

Copyright © 2006 by Stonesong Press, LLC

Facts On File, Inc.
132 West 31st Street
New York NY 10001

Library of Congress Cataloging-in-Publication Data

Wills, Charles.
    America in the 1950s / Charles A. Wills.
        p. cm. — (Decades of American history)
    "A Stonesong Press book."
    Includes bibliographical references and index.
    ISBN 0-8160-5640-4
  1. United States—History—1945–1953—Juvenile literature. 2. United
States—History—1953–1961—Juvenile literature. 3. Nineteen
fifties—Juvenile literature. I. Title. II. Series.
    E813.W47 2005
    973.921—dc22

                                                          2004018951

Text design by Laura Smyth, Smythetype
Photo research by Larry Schwartz
Cover design by Pehrsson Design

Printed in the United States of America

VB PKG 10 9 8 7 6 5 4 3 2 1

This book is printed on acid-free paper.

CONTENTS

CHAPTER 1

THE STATE OF THE NATION, 1950

The 48-star flag flew over the United States throughout the 1950s. *(Library of Congress)*

A PORTRAIT OF THE UNITED STATES IN 1950 showed a nation in transition, although many people feel that the decade was a quiet one. The U.S. census, taken every 10 years, provides an interesting snapshot of the United States at the midpoint of the 20th century.

The United States was home to about 151.5 million people as the 1950s began—an increase of more than 18 million since 1940. There were 48 stars on the flag in 1950, but by 1959, there were 50, as two territories, Alaska and Hawaii, became states.

Mom, dad, two kids, and the dog made up the "average American family" of the 1950s. *(Library of Congress)*

According to the 1950 census, white people accounted for almost 90 percent of the population, with African Americans accounting for about 10 percent. At this time the census did not record the races of Americans of Asian and Hispanic origins, though it is known that there were only about 320,000 Asian Americans and 340,000 American Indians living in the 48 states in the 1950s. (The figures for Asian Americans and American Indians would have been higher if the territories of Alaska and Hawaii had been included.)

Most Americans living in the 1950s had been born in the United States. Only about 7 percent of the U.S. population had been born overseas, mainly because Congress had passed laws in the 1920s that greatly limited immigration. The number of immigrants coming to the United States rose in the 1950s, but immigrants would not begin arriving in large numbers until the mid-1960s when Congress passed new laws opening up immigration.

In 1950 the United States was a nation in which many more people lived in urban areas (communities with more than 2,500 people) than ever before. Even before World War I, Americans had begun moving from farms to towns and cities. By 1950, only about one out of every three Americans lived in a rural area.

The city with the largest population in 1950 was New York, with nearly 8 million people. Chicago was second with about 3.5 million residents. Philadelphia came in third, with a little over 2 million people, though Los Angeles would rise to third place during the decade as its population increased from a little under 2 million to almost 2.5 million.

For all Americans, the most significant event of the 1940s was World War II, which the United States entered after the Japanese attack on Pearl Harbor in Hawaii on December 7, 1941. By the time the war ended in August 1945, about 16 million men and women had served in the armed forces, about half of them overseas. Some 400,000 gave their lives.

World War II changed the United States in many ways. During the war, millions of U.S. families moved from one part of the country to another as workers took

GIVE'EM HELL HARRY

Sadly, Franklin Roosevelt did not live to see the final victory over Germany and Japan—he died of a stroke on April 12, 1945. The only president to serve more than two back-to-back terms, Roosevelt had been in office since 1933 and was the only president many young Americans had ever known. His vice-president, former Missouri senator Harry Truman, was little known nationally when he took office upon Roosevelt's death. Some Americans worried that Truman was not up to leading the nation in such challenging times. Truman, however, proved a strong leader, especially in dealing with the Soviet Union. Yet, by the presidential election year of 1948, troubles with the Republican-controlled Congress and with members of his own Democratic Party made Truman unpopular with many Americans. Most politicians and journalists predicted an easy win for the Republican candidate, New York governor Thomas Dewey. Truman, however, was a fighter. Traveling by train, he crisscrossed the country making fiery speeches and earning the nickname "Give'em Hell Harry." Truman's plain speaking changed many voters' minds, and when the votes were counted in November, he won reelection in a surprise upset.

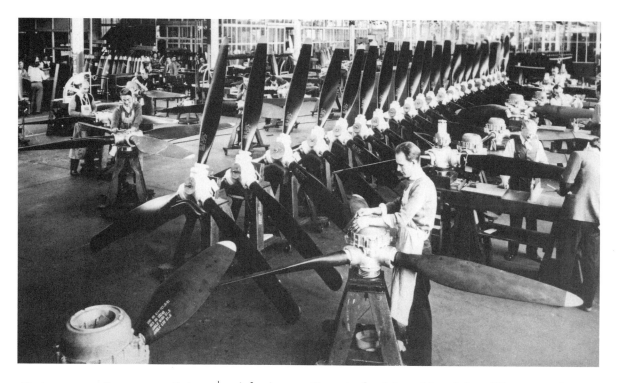

Airplane propellers come off the assembly line at a defense plant in this 1942 photograph. The U.S. war effort was backed up by millions of men and women working on the home front. *(Library of Congress)*

jobs in wartime industries. About 8 million people settled in the West Coast states of Oregon, Washington, and especially California, where there were many shipyards and aircraft plants needing workers. By the end of the 1940s, California had jumped ahead of Pennsylvania, Illinois, and Ohio to become the second most populous state. (New York was first.) Other western states, such as Arizona and Nevada, grew in population, too.

The war years also saw many people move from the South—the poorest part of the country at the time—to the big cities of the Northeast and Midwest. Among the migrants were hundreds of thousands of African Americans. They sought jobs and educational opportunities, and they hoped to escape the system of segregation in the South that made them second-class citizens in their own country.

Even outside of the South, however, African Americans often faced prejudice and inequality in jobs, housing, and education. During the war, tensions

JACKIE ROBINSON

One of the first victories in the fight for racial equality took place not in Congress or the courts, but on the baseball field. African-American players had been barred from major-league baseball in the 1880s, and they played in their own segregated, all-black leagues. By the 1940s, civil rights leaders demanded that major league baseball be integrated, with white and black players playing together. In 1947, Branch Rickey, president of the National League's Brooklyn Dodgers, broke baseball's color bar by hiring an African American.

The player he chose was Jackie Robinson. The grandson of a slave, Robinson had been a football star at the University of California at Los Angeles before switching to baseball, and he had served as an army officer in World War II. Despite threats and jeers, Robinson took to the field for his first game in September 1947. Named Rookie of the Year in his first season, Robinson went on to help the Dodgers win six pennants and a World Series. Along the way he changed the national pastime forever.

Jackie Robinson backed up his presence on the field with impressive statistics: He batted .297 in his first season. (*Library of Congress*)

between whites and African Americans led to riots in New York City and Detroit that left more than 40 people dead.

THE WARTIME BOOM

As the 1940s began, the U.S. economy was stuck in a depression that had begun in 1929. Although conditions were not as bad in 1939 as they had been at the height of the Great Depression in the mid-1930s, one in every 10 U.S. workers was without a job in 1940. The United States began to come out of the Great Depression after the start of World War II in Europe in September 1939. Although most Americans hoped that the United States would stay out of the war, the country began building up its defenses and sending aid to the nations fighting Nazi Germany. As a result, factories that had been shuttered for a decade roared back into life.

After the Japanese attack on Pearl Harbor brought the United States into the worldwide struggle against Nazi Germany and Japan, U.S. industries went into high gear. There was a job for anyone who wanted one

"I'm not concerned with your liking or disliking me... All I ask is that you respect me as a human being."

—Jackie Robinson to his 1947 Brooklyn Dodgers teammates

An African American works at the Douglas Aircraft Company's Los Angeles, California, plant during World War II. In 1941, President Franklin Roosevelt signed an Executive Order making it illegal for the defense industry to discriminate against African Americans in hiring. *(Library of Congress)*

as the nation's mills, plants, and factories manufactured planes, tanks, trucks, and thousands of other products needed by the U.S. military and by the forces of its allies, Britain and, after June 1941, the Soviet Union. With so many men in uniform, millions of women entered the workforce for the first time.

After the war ended in August 1945, many Americans feared that the economic boom of the war years would end and that many of the millions of U.S. veterans would not be able to find jobs when they came home from overseas. The boom continued, however, as factories once again produced consumer goods, such as cars and appliances.

Americans had the money to buy these products, too, because production of many consumer goods had stopped during the war. With few products available, many Americans had saved their money. With the war over, they were ready to spend. The prosperous times that began during the war continued for the next 30 years.

THE WAR CHANGES U.S. SOCIETY

In 1944, Congress passed a far-reaching law known as the G.I. Bill. The law provided money for returning veterans to pay for education and job training. It also guaranteed mortgages (loans to buy homes) for veterans, at a low rate of interest.

As a result, millions of veterans and their families were able to buy their own homes. Many veterans chose to buy houses in the suburbs—communities close to but separate from major cities.

The end of the war also began the era that would become known as the Baby Boom. The U.S. birth rate rose in 1946 as veterans got married and started families, and it continued to rise until about 1964. About 75 million children were born in those years.

For millions of women, the end of the war meant leaving the workforce and returning to more traditional roles as full-time wives and mothers. During the war, the government told women it was their patriotic duty to enter the workforce to take the places of men entering military service. After the war, women were told it was their duty to leave their jobs to free them up for returning veterans.

Many women were happy to return to the kind of life they had led before the war. Others, however, missed the independence and sense of accomplishment they had gained in the wartime workforce, when they had proved they could do a man's job, despite the doubts of some traditionally minded Americans.

FROM WORLD WAR TO COLD WAR

World War II not only changed U.S. society; it changed the role of the United States in the world. The war was the most deadly, costly conflict in history. Perhaps as many as 60 million people worldwide died as a result

"From Stettin in the Baltic to Trieste in the Adriatic, an iron curtain has descended across the Continent."

—Winston Churchill, at Westminster College, 1946

German children wave as an American transport plane comes in for a landing at Berlin's Tempelhof Airport. During the 321 days of the Berlin blockade, U.S. and British planes carried 2.5 million tons of supplies into the city's Allied zones. *(Library of Congress)*

Hungry Polish children line up to receive food aid from the United States in the aftermath of World War II. British statesman Winston Churchill described the devastation of Europe in a 1946 speech: "Over wide areas...tormented, hungry, care-worn and bewildered human beings gape at the ruins of their cities and homes, and scan the dark horizons for the approach of some new peril, tyranny, or terror." *(Library of Congress)*

of the war, most of them civilians. Much of Europe and Asia was in ruins, and millions of people were hungry and homeless.

The war weakened the winning nations as well as the losers. The Soviet Union's struggle against Germany caused the deaths of 20 million Soviet citizens and destroyed large parts of Soviet territory. Britain's government was out of money by the war's end, and its once-mighty world-wide empire soon began to fall apart.

In contrast, the war made the United States a much stronger and more powerful country. No invading armies had fought on its soil. No enemy bombers had rained death and destruction on its cities. The nation's farms and factories were not only undamaged, they were producing more than ever before. The United States was now not just a world power—it was a superpower. The United States was also the only nation to possess the world's most powerful weapon—the atomic bomb.

Even before the end of World War II, the United States found itself involved in a new conflict—one that would become known as the cold war. When Germany surrendered in 1945, Soviet forces occupied much of Central and Eastern Europe, including the nations of Poland, Hungary, Czechoslovakia, Romania, Bulgaria, and Yugoslavia, as well as the eastern half of Germany. During the war, Soviet dictator Joseph Stalin promised to allow free elections in these countries (except for Germany) so that they could choose their own governments.

After the war's end, however, Stalin and other Soviet leaders broke their promises and installed communist governments in the countries the Soviet Union occupied. In addition, the Soviets supported communist movements elsewhere in Europe.

In a speech at Westminster College in Fulton, Missouri, in March 1946, former British prime minister Winston Churchill described how, in his phrase, "an Iron Curtain" had fallen across Europe. On one side of the curtain were Britain, France, the Netherlands, and other European nations with democratically elected governments, which were friendly with the United States. On the other side were the communist countries whose governments were closely allied with the Soviet Union.

With the horrors of World War II still fresh in people's minds, few Americans or Europeans wanted a full-scale war with the Soviet Union. Nevertheless, many people, including U.S. president Harry Truman, believed that the democratic nations had to stand up to the Soviets, or they might take over all of Europe and spread communism throughout the world.

In 1947, Truman made an important speech in which he asked Congress to provide military aid to the governments of Greece and Turkey, which were fighting Soviet-supported communist rebels. Congress agreed. This was the start of a U.S. policy called containment, which was intended to halt the spread of communism in Europe and elsewhere. The policy of containment did not exclude war.

Later that year, Secretary of State George Marshall announced that the United States would help rebuild the war-shattered economies of the European nations. In 1948, under the Marshall Plan, the United States provided $23 billion in aid to 16 countries. The program helped convince Europeans that the United States was committed to Europe's security, freedom, and prosperity.

Also in 1948, the Soviet Union tested the U.S. commitment to Europe. After Germany's surrender in 1945, the United States, Britain, and France occupied the western part of Germany while the Soviets occupied the eastern part. The four nations also jointly occupied

"America was not built on fear. America was built on courage, on imagination and an unbeatable determination to do the job at hand."
—Harry S. Truman, Jan. 1, 1947, special message to Congress

A smiling Harry Truman speaks from his train during his so-called whistlestop campaign. The president stopped at towns and cities across the country to criticize what he called the "do-nothing, good-for-nothing" Republican-dominated Congress. *(Library of Congress)*

Born to an American mother and an English father, Winston Churchill (1874–1965) led Great Britain through World War II and warned of the dangers of Soviet expansion. *(Library of Congress)*

General George Marshall (1880–1959) was appointed secretary of state in January 1947. *(Library of Congress)*

Germany's largest city, Berlin, although Berlin was located in Soviet-occupied eastern Germany. In June, the Soviets halted all road and rail traffic from West Germany to Berlin. As a result, the people of West Berlin (the part of the city controlled by the United States, Britain, and France) were cut off from shipments of food, fuel, and other supplies coming from the West.

For more than a year, U.S. and British military pilots flew supplies into West Berlin in an around-the-clock operation known as the Berlin Airlift. Finally, in May 1949, the Soviets backed down and reopened the roads to Berlin.

While the Berlin Airlift was going on, the United States, Canada, and seven European nations formed the North Atlantic Treaty Organization, or NATO, in April 1949. All the NATO countries pledged to support one another in the event of an attack on any member nation.

The cold war grew chillier in September 1949, when the Soviet Union exploded an atomic bomb. The United States had not expected the Soviet Union to develop such a complex weapon so quickly. (It turned out that the Soviets had help from agents spying in the United States.) The Soviet bomb raised the awful possibility of a nuclear war between the United States and the Soviet Union. A month later, a communist government came to power in China, leading to fears that communism would spread throughout Asia as well as Europe. Holding the line against communism while avoiding all-out war—especially nuclear war—would be the greatest challenge facing the United States in the decade ahead.

CHAPTER 2

McCARTHYISM AND KOREA, 1950–1952

ON FEBRUARY 22, 1950, JOSEPH McCarthy, Republican senator from Wisconsin, gave a speech to the Republican Women's Club of Wheeling, West Virginia. "I have here in my hand," he began, "a list of 205…names that were known to the Secretary of State as being members of the Communist Party and who nevertheless are still working and shaping policy in the State Department."

Senator Joseph McCarthy speaks on the radio. McCarthy's reckless accusations against suspected communists gave the English language a new word— "McCarthyism." *(Library of Congress)*

TRUMAN UNDER ATTACK

In 1950, President Truman signed legislation that allowed the people of the territory of Puerto Rico—the Caribbean island ruled by the United States since 1898—to establish their own constitution. Puerto Rican Nationalists, who wanted complete independence from the United States, opposed the law, and a handful of extreme Nationalists turned to terrorism. On November 1, 1950, two Nationalist terrorists tried to break into Washington, D.C.'s Blair House, where President Truman was living while part of the White House was being rebuilt, to assassinate the president.

Although Truman escaped harm, a fierce gun battle broke out between the would-be assassins and Secret Service agents and D.C. police, leaving one Nationalist and one police officer dead. In 1951, a majority of Puerto Ricans voted to stay within the United States as a self-governing commonwealth, and on July 25, 1952, Puerto Rico's new constitution was officially established. Yet the unrest continued. In 1954, Nationalist terrorists struck again, this time opening fire on legislators in the U.S. House of Representatives, wounding five members of Congress.

"I am most willing to answer all questions about myself...But to hurt innocent people whom I knew many years ago in order to save myself is, to me, inhuman and indecent and dishonorable."

—Writer Lillian Hellman, 1952

McCarthy was a little-known figure at the start of the 1950s, but his Wheeling speech made him famous overnight. Born in 1908, McCarthy served with the U.S. Marines in World War II, and he claimed to be a war hero but in fact saw little combat. Switching from the Democratic Party to the Republican Party, he was elected to the U.S. Senate in 1946.

From 1950 through 1954, McCarthy accused many people in government of being communist agents working against U.S. interests. To his many supporters, McCarthy was a patriot and a hero. To his critics, including those in his own Republican Party, McCarthy was an irresponsible man who made wild accusations, usually with no evidence, to boost his political career.

In July 1951, a senate panel called McCarthy's charges about communists in the State Department "false" and "a fraud." McCarthy, however, continued his accusations. Although he could rarely support his charges with evidence, communist spies really had been at work in the United States. Just before McCarthy's Wheeling speech, a jury found that Alger Hiss, a former State Department official, had lied about his ties to U.S. communists spying for the Soviet Union. (Hiss, who died in 1996, always claimed to be innocent, but documents uncovered in the former Soviet Union contain evidence showing that he probably was a spy.)

A few weeks after the Wheeling speech, British officials arrested scientist Klaus Fuchs for spying on behalf of the Soviet Union. During World War II, Fuchs had worked on the U.S. atomic bomb project at Los Alamos, New Mexico. In 1950, he revealed that several Americans, who were members of a Soviet spy ring, had helped him pass secrets to the Soviets.

One member of the spy ring revealed that Julius and Ethel Rosenberg, a married couple from New York, had also been spying for the Soviets. In March 1951, the Rosenbergs were found guilty of conspiracy to commit espionage (spying) and were sentenced to death. (The Rosenbergs were executed in the electric chair on June 19, 1953.)

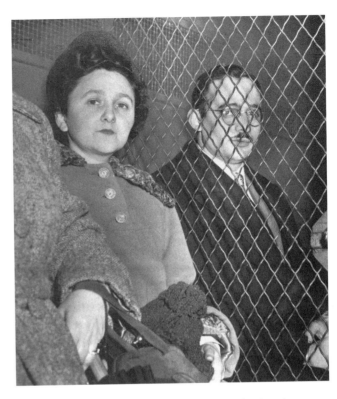

Separated by a wire barrier, Julius and Ethel Rosenberg leave the federal courthouse in New York City after their conviction for spying. Many people in the United States and around the world protested their execution. *(Library of Congress)*

These real-life spy cases had the unfortunate effect of making McCarthy's talk of "communist conspiracies" believable to many Americans. These cases also encouraged the work of the House Committee on Un-American Activities (HUAC).

Throughout the late 1940s and 1950s HUAC investigated what it called "communist influence" in the movie industry, the nation's universities, and the scientific community. Although HUAC did find some instances of Communist influence in these areas, it never found a major conspiracy against the U.S. government.

Some people had their careers and reputations ruined by their appearances before HUAC. Hollywood actors and screenwriters who refused to cooperate with HUAC, for example, were often "blacklisted," or refused work, by movie studios. On the other hand, those who did cooperate by identifying movie industry figures, who had been in the past or were then sympathetic to

Alger Hiss served as a law clerk on the U.S. Supreme Court and rose to high rank in the State Department before his conviction for perjury in 1950. He served three years of a five-year prison sentence. *(Library of Congress)*

communism, found themselves hated by those who had not "named names," and by those who were named as communists, often mistakenly or unfairly.

McCarthy and HUAC created a climate of fear and mistrust among Americans. During this Red Scare, many people were afraid to express unpopular opinions or criticize the government out of fear of being identified as communist.

POLICE ACTION IN KOREA

In June 1950, the cold war heated up suddenly in Korea, a place few Americans knew much about. A small peninsula to the east of China, Korea was ruled by Japan from 1910 until 1945. After Japan's defeat in World War II, Soviet forces occupied the northern part of the peninsula, and U.S. troops occupied the southern part. The 38th parallel (line of latitude) served as the dividing line between the two zones.

After U.S. and Soviet troops withdrew from Korea in 1948, it was divided into two nations: the People's

American soldiers patrol the hills of Korea. The peninsula's rugged terrain and extreme summer heat and winter cold made military operations very difficult. *(Library of Congress)*

Democratic Republic of Korea (North Korea), and the Republic of Korea (South Korea). Ruled by Kim Il-sung, North Korea was an independent communist country that had close ties to the Soviet Union. The United States supported Syngman Rhee as the leader of South Korea.

With Soviet approval and support, the North Korean People's Army attacked South Korea on June 25, 1950. Kim Il-sung's goal was to conquer South Korea and to reunite the two Koreas into a single communist nation.

At an emergency meeting, the United Nations Security Council protested North Korea's invasion of South Korea. (This vote was possible only because the Soviet Union, a Security Council member with veto power, was absent. At the time, the Soviets were boycotting the council because it refused to recognize the People's Republic of China, a new communist nation, as a member.) The United Nations also passed a resolution authorizing member nations to help South Korea repel the invaders.

The military forces of several nations fought on behalf of South Korea under the UN flag. The main source of help for South Korea, however, was the United States.

On June 30, 1950, President Harry Truman announced that the United States would send forces to South Korea. "To return to the rule of force in international affairs would have far-reaching effects," said the president. "The United States will continue to uphold international law." Truman, however, did not ask Congress to declare war on North Korea. In fact, he avoided using the word war altogether. According to the president, the conflict in Korea was a "police action."

On July 7, General Douglas MacArthur was appointed commander of UN forces in Korea (U.S. troops accounted for 90 percent of these troops.) MacArthur was one of the most distinguished soldiers in the United States, with a career spanning a half-century. He led U.S. forces in the South Pacific in World War II and then ruled

General Douglas MacArthur poses with his trademark corncob pipe. He took command of UN forces in Korea in 1950. *(Library of Congress)*

CHOPPERS TO THE RESCUE

Although helicopters saw limited service toward the end of World War II, the Korean War was the first conflict in which these aircraft played an important role. Unlike fixed-wing aircraft, which need a long, smooth runway for take off and landing, helicopters can take off and land almost anywhere—something especially important in the rugged, hilly landscape of Korea. Choppers, so called for the sound that their rotary blades make, rescued downed pilots from behind enemy lines. Helicopters carried the wounded quickly from the front lines to Mobile Army Surgical Hospitals— the MASH units later made famous by a movie and television series. Serving as flying trucks, helicopters also carried supplies and troops. The most widely used helicopters in Korea were the Sikorsky H-5 Dragonfly, the Bell H-13, and the Hiller H-23.

Japan during the U.S. occupation. In 1950, at the age of 70, the legendary general had another war to win.

The North Korean army outnumbered the South Korean army and had plenty of Soviet-supplied tanks and aircraft. The South Koreans could not hold back the invaders. MacArthur rushed U.S. troops to South Korea from Japan, but the Americans were inexperienced and unprepared for combat. In their first battles against the North Koreans, many U.S. soldiers were killed or captured.

By September 1950, the North Koreans had captured the South Korean capital of Seoul and had driven the South Korean and U.S. forces into a pocket around the port city of Pusan in the southern part of the peninsula. Only U.S. air power kept the North Koreans from overrunning all of South Korea.

MacArthur then gambled on a risky operation. He planned a U.S. landing by marines and soldiers behind the enemy's lines at Inchon, a port on Korea's western coast about 25 miles from Seoul. To succeed, the landing force would need to achieve a complete surprise and perfect timing.

The gamble paid off. On September 15, a fleet of 200 ships put U.S. forces ashore at Inchon. Driving inland, they recaptured Seoul after heavy fighting with

A weary, unshaven American infantryman in Korea reads mail from home. About 1.5 million American men and women served in the Korean conflict.
(Library of Congress)

Thanks to quick evacuation by helicopter, many soldiers wounded in the fighting in Korea survived injuries that would have been fatal in earlier wars. *(Library of Congress)*

the North Koreans on September 26. Meanwhile, U.S. and South Korean units in the south moved northward. Caught between the two forces, the North Korean army crumbled, and its survivors began retreating northward into North Korea.

The combined UN forces then crossed the 38th parallel and entered North Korea. They continued advancing toward the Yalu River, which formed the border between North Korea and the region of Manchuria in China. The Chinese government warned that if U.S.

General Matthew Ridgway (1895–1993) led U.S. airborne troops in World War II. After succeeding Douglas MacArthur as United Nations commander in Korea, Ridgway conducted a skillful defense against the Chinese and North Korean forces. *(Library of Congress)*

"'Old soldiers never die; they just fade away'…And like the old soldier of that ballad, I now close my military career and just fade away, an old soldier who tried to do his duty as God gave him the light to see that duty. Good-bye."

—General Douglas MacArthur's
farewell speech
to Congress, 1951

troops reached the Yalu, China might enter the war to assist North Korea. MacArthur ignored the warnings and continued the advance, despite the fact that U.S. soldiers were now sometimes fighting Chinese troops.

On November 26, the Chinese launched a major attack against UN forces. In bitterly cold weather, the U.S. First Marine Division, together with U.S. and British army units, managed to fight its way from the Chosin Reservoir to safety at the port of Hungnam on Korea's eastern coast. It was a brilliant feat, but it did not disguise the fact that UN forces were in serious trouble.

The situation got worse on December 31, when about 500,000 Chinese troops began pushing UN forces back into South Korea. Once again, U.S. air power held up the Communists, and by April the reinforced UN army drove the North Koreans and Chinese north of the 38th parallel.

MacArthur now wanted to expand the war by bombing Chinese airfields in Manchuria and by using the U.S. Navy to block the flow of supplies into Chinese ports. President Truman would not allow these actions. The president did not want to risk the Soviet Union entering the conflict on China's side. Neither did the top U.S. military commander, General Omar Bradley, Chairman of the Joint Chiefs of Staff, who told Truman that taking the war into China would involve the United States in "the wrong war, at the wrong place, at the wrong time, and with the wrong enemy."

Nevertheless, MacArthur openly challenged Truman's war policies in letters and speeches. The general's public criticism of the president—his commander-in-chief—was unacceptable to Truman. On April 11, 1951, he fired MacArthur for repeatedly challenging the president's authority, replacing him with General Matthew Ridgway. As Truman put it when he announced that he was relieving MacArthur of command, "If I allow him to defy the civil authority, I would myself be violating my oath to defend the Constitution."

MacArthur returned to a hero's welcome in the United States. Many people agreed with MacArthur's wish to extend the war, believing that Truman had wronged a great man. MacArthur's popularity increased after he made an emotional speech to Congress before retiring from the army. Some people thought he might run for public office and had a chance of winning the Republican presidential nomination in 1952. MacArthur's popularity, however, never turned into major political support.

On July 10, 1951, peace talks aimed at ending the Korean War began. The military forces in the field, however, continued to fight as the talks dragged on. Two years would go by before the war finally ended.

THE LONG BOOM CONTINUES

On December 16, 1950, when the fighting in Korea was at its height, President Truman declared a "state of national emergency," telling Americans that they must "put aside…personal interests for the good of the country." In practice, this declaration announced the president's decision to raise taxes to pay for the war in Korea and to place government controls on wages and prices to halt inflation.

Truman later announced a big increase in government spending, almost all of it on the military. These measures—especially the tax increases—were not

HARLEY EARL

No one had more to do with the look of U.S. products in the 1950s than industrial designer Harley Earl. Earl began his career customizing cars for movie stars in Hollywood. He then started work at General Motors Art and Color Department in 1927. It was in the 1950s that Earl really hit his stride, introducing chrome and tailfins to cars and designing such classic vehicles as the LeSabre, the Corvette, and the Corvair. Earl's masterpiece was the massive 1959 Cadillac, a car with tailfins "sharp enough to fillet passers-by," in the words of writers Jane and Michael Stern. Some 50 million drivers bought Earl-designed cars in the 1950s. Although remembered mostly for his cars, Earl's other design innovations included food in aerosol cans and roll-on deodorant.

popular with many Americans, including the Republicans in Congress. While most Republicans and Democrats agreed that the United States needed to strengthen its defenses in the face of the communist threat, Republicans believed that the larger budget would increase the federal budget deficit and weaken the economy.

Truman was widely criticized for two other wartime actions. In August 1950, he ordered the federal government to take control of the nation's railroads when a planned strike by railroad workers threatened to hold up the transport of war materials around the nation. In April 1952, he took control of the nation's steel mills, once again because of a strike threat. In June 1952, however, the Supreme Court ruled that Truman had gone beyond the Constitution's limits on presidential power in seizing the steel mills.

As it turned out, the Korean War did not slow down the economic boom that had begun during World War II. Prices did rise for a time, and after the war there was a brief recession in 1954–55, when the jobless rate went from about 3 percent to about 5 percent. The recession did not last long, however.

The rise in defense spending actually boosted the overall economy. By the end of the 1950s, the U.S. government was the biggest single customer for the

SPECIAL ADDED ATTRACTION

In the 1950s, Las Vegas, Nevada, went from being a sleepy desert town to one of the nation's most popular vacation destinations, thanks to the construction of gambling casinos. In 1951, visitors to Las Vegas could not only gamble, drink, and dance but also view a nuclear explosion. Early that year the Atomic Energy Commission tested five atomic bombs in the Nevada desert just 50 miles from the city. One newspaper called the blasts "the greatest tourist lure since the nickel slot machine," but casino workers reported that many people did not even bother to leave the gaming tables to watch the blasts.

nation's largest companies. Firms such as Boeing, Remington-Rand, General Electric, Raytheon, and McDonnell-Douglas made huge profits as they turned out the aircraft, warships, and countless other products needed by the U.S. military. Plenty of smaller companies shared in the defense boom: By 1955, more than 40,000 U.S. firms had contracts with the U.S. government.

In fact, the 1950s would be remembered as a one of the most prosperous decades in U.S. history—the start of the so-called long boom. The decade was a time of relatively low unemployment and high wages and salaries. Real wages (adjusted for inflation) rose by more

Factory workers punch a time clock after their workday. Despite occasional recessions, unemployment remained low during the 1950s. *(Library of Congress)*

WELCOME, CHARLIE BROWN

On October 2, 1950, the Peanuts daily comic strip first appeared in newspapers. Written and drawn by 27-year-old Charles Schulz, Peanuts chronicled the adventures (or misadventures) of a group of children, including Charlie Brown, Lucy and Linus Van Pelt, and of course, Charlie Brown's dog, Snoopy. Warm and witty, Peanuts and its unique characters became a beloved part of U.S. popular culture. Schulz continued to draw Peanuts right up until his death in 2000.

Cartoonist Charles Schulz shares a drink with his dog Spike—the canine that provided the inspiration for Snoopy. *(Library of Congress)*

than 50 percent between 1950 and 1960. Many Americans who worked in factories and shops were now able to enjoy a middle-class lifestyle, which included home ownership, a decent car (or two), and enough money left over to pay for vacations, send their children to college, and save for retirement.

With steady work and bigger paychecks, Americans could afford a wide variety of consumer goods—from cars and televisions to labor-saving appliances, such as dishwashers and washing machines.

As businesses expanded, more and more Americans were able to move from blue-collar jobs on the shop floor or on the assembly line to white-collar jobs as managers or technicians. In 1950, only 9 percent of U.S. households had a middle-class income of $10,000 or more per year. By 1960, the number was more than 30 percent.

Not everyone shared in this prosperity. Although millions of Americans joined the ranks of the middle class in the 1950s, the gap between the wealthiest and the poorest Americans widened. By 1960, the wealthiest 5 percent of the U.S. population accounted for more than 14 percent of the nation's income, while the poorest 20 percent of Americans accounted for only about 5 percent.

THE CAR CULTURE AND THE JET AGE

Car production and sales played a big part in keeping the long boom going. In 1950, U.S. automakers produced 6.7 million cars. In 1955, the decade's peak year for car production, that figure jumped to 9.2 million cars. General Motors, the biggest car maker, rolled out 2.8 million cars in 1955, for total sales of $10 billion. By 1960, the height of the boom was over, though car production remained strong at 7.9 million.

Throughout the decade, U.S. auto manufacturers produced about two-thirds of all the vehicles made in the world. And although countries such as Japan and Germany greatly increased their car production in the 1950s, U.S. drivers preferred U.S. cars by a wide margin. At the end of the decade, imported cars accounted for only 8 percent of U.S. auto sales; half of those imports were Volkswagen Beetles.

Although the United States became a car-oriented culture after Henry Ford introduced the Model T in the early 1900s, the car became an even more important

"See the U.S.A. in your Chevrolet!"

—1950s advertising slogan

The so-called Big Three carmakers—Chrysler, Ford, and General Motors—dominated the U.S. auto industry in the 1950s. By the end of the decade, many of the smaller independent carmakers—like Kaiser-Frazer, manufacturers of the models shown in this 1950 ad—had gone out of business. *(Private Collection)*

Dick and Mac McDonald opened their first quick service restaurant in 1948. Seven years later, salesman Ray Kroc convinced the brothers to let him expand the small chain through a system of franchises. Shown here is Kroc's first McDonald's, in Des Plaines, Illinois. It is now a museum. *(Library of Congress)*

part of American society in the 1950s. Cars were a necessity in the suburbs, which were becoming home to a majority of Americans. By the 1950s, three out of four U.S. families owned at least one car, and many families owned two or more cars.

New businesses sprang up to serve the flourishing car culture. There were drive-in movie theaters (more than 4,000 by the end of the decade), drive-in restaurants, drive-in banks, and even drive-in churches. Fast-food restaurants began to appear along the nation's roadsides. These eateries included the McDonald's chain, which started with a single restaurant in San Bernardino, California. McDonald's grew to 228 locations across the country by 1960.

Because most U.S. workers had paid vacations, more and more families took to the road each year. In 1951, business owner Kemmons Wilson took his family on a cross-country trip. Disgusted at having to stay at dirty, overpriced motels, Wilson decided to start a nationwide chain of motels that offered clean, standardized rooms at budget prices, with children staying for free. The first Holiday Inn opened in Memphis, Tennessee, in 1952; a decade later, there were 400. Along with the golden arches of McDonald's restaurants, the neon arrow Great Sign of the Holiday Inn motel chain became a familiar roadside sight in the 1950s.

CHAPTER 3

"I LIKE IKE," 1952–1954

PRESIDENT TRUMAN CHOSE NOT TO run for another term in 1952. The Democratic nomination went to Illinois governor Adlai Stevenson, with Senator John Sparkman of Alabama as his running mate.

The Republican candidate was one of the most popular and respected figures in the United States— Dwight D. Eisenhower. "Ike," as he was nicknamed, had

Dwight Eisenhower (second from right) and Richard Nixon and their wives, Patricia Ryan Nixon and Mamie Doud Eisenhower, celebrate at the Republican Convention in Philadelphia. The 1952 conventions were the first to be broadcast on national television. *(AP/Wide World)*

Richard Nixon with Checkers, the cocker spaniel made famous by the vice-presidential candidate's televised speech. *(AP/Wide World)*

"Dick, you're my boy!"

—Republican presidential candidate Dwight D. Eisenhower to his running mate, Senator Richard Nixon, after the Checkers speech, September 1952

commanded the Allied forces in Europe during World War II. After the war, he served briefly as president of Columbia University in New York City and then as commander of NATO. Eisenhower's running mate was California senator Richard Nixon, who had won national fame for investigating accused communists as a member of the House Committee on Un-American Activities (HUAC).

During the 1952 campaign, the Republicans played on Eisenhower's tremendous popularity with the campaign slogan, "I Like Ike." They concentrated on the themes of "Korea, Communism, and Corruption." Republican politicians accused the Truman administration of letting the war in Korea drag on. They charged that Democratic politicians were not doing enough to combat the communist threat at home and overseas, and that members of the Democratic administration were dishonest.

Before long, however, the Republicans had to answer charges of dishonesty aimed at them by the Democrats. Nixon was accused of accepting gifts in return for political favors. As the scandal grew, Eisenhower considered asking Nixon to withdraw his candidacy.

Nixon took the bold step of appearing on national television to defend himself. In an emotional speech, he denied wrongdoing but said that he had accepted a dog named Checkers as a gift from a political supporter. "And you know," Nixon went on, "the kids [Nixon's two daughters], like all kids, love the dog, and I just want to say this, right now, that regardless of what they say about it, we're going to keep it."

Nixon's television appearance was a success. Eisenhower kept Nixon on the ticket, and the so-called Checkers speech showed the growing importance of television in U.S. politics.

When Americans went to the polls in November, the result was a landslide for Eisenhower and the Republicans. Eisenhower won with 34 million votes as opposed to 27.3

million for Stevenson. The Republicans also became the majority party in both houses of Congress.

Uneasy Peace in Korea

During the campaign, Eisenhower promised that if elected, he would travel to Korea in an effort to make peace. After his victory, Eisenhower did go to Korea to meet with the commanders of UN forces, but the conflict continued.

Although peace talks had begun in mid-1951, they were going nowhere. The main sticking point involved the prisoners of war. North Korea demanded that UN forces release all North Korean prisoners, but about 50,000 prisoners did not want to return to their Communist homeland.

The ongoing fighting in Korea was the biggest issue in the 1952 presidential election. Here, American forces watch a shell explode. *(Library of Congress)*

BRAINWASHED?

U.S. troops captured by the Chinese and North Koreans endured terrible conditions in prisoner-of-war camps—scanty food, inadequate medical care, and beatings and other abuse. In addition to these physical hardships, some U.S. prisoners also endured a form of mental abuse that came to be called brainwashing, from the Chinese phrase meaning "cleansing the mind." To brainwash prisoners in the Korean War, they were kept awake for long periods while guards lectured them about communism and urged them to confess their war crimes. The purpose was to destroy the prisoners' loyalty to the United States so that they would accept the superiority of communism. Some prisoners signed confessions, but most of them did so only to stop the terrible treatment. When the war ended, however, 21 U.S. prisoners of war decided to go to China rather than return home. There are differing accounts of their fates, but at least one was still living in China in the 1980s.

While the peace talks dragged on, UN and North Korean and Chinese forces continued to fight along the 38th parallel. The battles of 1952–53 were smaller than the big clashes of 1950–51, but Americans continued to be killed and wounded, making the war more and more unpopular at home.

After the death of Soviet dictator Joseph Stalin in March 1953, North Korea's representatives at the peace talks were more willing to negotiate. Eisenhower also kept the pressure on the communists by making it known that the United States might bomb military sites in China unless an agreement was reached.

U.S. and Korean diplomats sign the agreement that finally brought an end to the Korean War, in Panmunjom, a small village about three miles south of the 38th Parallel, which divides North Korea from South Korea. *(Library of Congress)*

Finally, in July 1953, North Korea agreed to a truce, and the guns fell silent. The Korean peninsula remained divided between a communist-ruled North Korea and a democratic South. To guard against another invasion of South Korea, thousands of U.S. troops were stationed along the demilitarized zone (DMZ) that separated the two Koreas—a situation that continues in the 21st century.

About 33,000 Americans died in the Korean War, with more than 135,000 troops seriously wounded, captured, or missing. While most Americans accepted that the United States had to act against the communist invasion of South Korea, the war had been long and costly, and it ended without a clear victory. Few celebrations marked the announcement of the truce. The Korean War would eventually become known as "America's Forgotten War." It was not until 1995, for example, that a national memorial to those who had served and died in Korea was dedicated in Washington, D.C.

Grandson of one secretary of state and the nephew of another, John Foster Dulles (1888–1959) served as Eisenhower's secretary of state from 1953 until a month before his death. *(Library of Congress)*

EISENHOWER'S FOREIGN POLICY

The new president continued the policy of supporting countries fighting communist movements. His secretary of state, John Foster Dulles, wanted to go even further. Dulles believed that the United States should not just contain communism but should also try to roll back communist gains wherever it could. Eisenhower, however, tried to steer a more moderate course. In addition to the danger of sparking a war with the Soviet Union or China, Eisenhower was also concerned that too much military spending might weaken the nation's economy.

The Eisenhower administration was especially worried about the situation in French Indochina, the lands in Southeast Asia that were under French rule (Vietnam, Laos, and Cambodia). In French-ruled Vietnam, communist guerrillas, the Viet-Minh, were fighting for independence from French colonial rule.

President Eisenhower's firm belief in collective security led to the founding of defense alliances such as the Southeast Asia Treaty Organization (SEATO) and, in 1955, the Central Treaty Organization (CENTO), which included Iran, Iraq, Turkey, and Pakistan. *(Library of Congress)*

"You have a row of dominoes set up..."

—President Eisenhower,
April 7, 1954

By the early 1950s, the United States was supplying most of the weapons, aircraft, and other supplies used by the French forces in Indochina. President Eisenhower defended U.S. aid to the French in a press conference in April 1954. Eisenhower said that if one country in Southeast Asia fell to communism, the others would follow like a row of dominoes. This idea became known as the domino theory.

Later that year, the Viet-Minh surrounded a large French force at a base called Dien Bien Phu in Vietnam. The French asked the United States to send warplanes against the Viet-Minh. Although some of the president's advisers wanted to provide this air support to the French, Eisenhower decided against it. The president knew that U.S. intervention might bring the Chinese into the conflict, as it had in Korea. The president was also aware that despite the anticommunist feelings of most Americans, few people wanted to get into a war in this remote part of the world.

After the defeat at Dien Bien Phu, the French withdrew from Indochina. Like Korea, Vietnam was then divided into two nations—a communist-ruled North Vietnam and a U.S.-backed South Vietnam. According to the agreement that ended the conflict, the two Vietnams were to be reunited after free elections to decide the kind of government the country was to have.

Toward the end of 1954, the United States joined Britain, France, Australia, New Zealand, the Philippines, Pakistan, and Thailand to form the Southeast Asia Treaty Organization (SEATO). The organization was set up as an Asian counterpart to NATO as part of the effort to keep communism from spreading in the region.

Military aid and alliances such as SEATO were one way in which the United States sought to contain communism. Covert (secret) operations were another. In 1947, Congress had established the Central Intelligence Agency (CIA). The CIA's purpose was to gather and distribute information to government leaders about threats to national security. The agency, however, also conducted secret operations overseas against movements that were thought to be unfriendly to the United States.

The first such operation took place in 1953 in the oil-rich nation of Iran, where the CIA supported a group that removed the nation's procommunist premier, Mohammad Mosaddeq, from power. Mossadeq's government had taken over Iran's oil industry, and the U.S. government was concerned that the flow of oil would stop. A year later, a CIA-backed group overthrew another procommunist government in the Central American country of Guatemala.

Although the details of these operations were secret, it was widely known that the CIA had a hand in the Iranian and Guatemalan coups, or overthrows, and that the agency was involved in similar operations elsewhere. This development worried some Americans, because the agency was permitted to operate outside of the control of Congress. Other citizens were concerned that the CIA's operations would tarnish the image of the United States around the world.

BROWN V. BOARD OF EDUCATION

President Eisenhower's first term saw the first big victory in the fight for civil rights for African Americans. Starting around the time of World War I (1914–18), millions of African Americans began moving from the segregated South to cities in the North and West. Even outside the South, African Americans faced discrimination in jobs, housing, and education. (This treatment is often called de facto segregation—segregation in fact, although not in law).

Despite the discrimination in northern cities such as New York, Chicago, and Detroit, African Americans could vote in the North and use the same public facilities as whites. Many African Americans asked why they could sit alongside whites on a bus or in a restaurant in

I PLEDGE ALLEGIANCE…
In June 1954, Congress passed a resolution that added the words "under God" to the Pledge of Allegiance, which is spoken by millions of U.S. schoolchildren every morning. The change was a sign of the importance of religion to Americans in the 1950s. Although critics charged that Americans were more interested in money and possessions than spiritual concerns, church and synagogue memberships rose during the decade, and evangelists such as Billy Graham attracted huge audiences across the country. Books such as Fulton Oursler's *The Greatest Story Ever Told* (1949) and Norman Vincent Peale's *The Power of Positive Thinking* (1952) were best sellers, as was the Revised Standard Version of the Bible—the top-selling nonfiction book in the country from 1952 through 1954. Some Americans believed the change to the Pledge was unconstitutional because the new wording went against the separation of church and state established in the First Amendment to the Constitution.

"We conclude that in the field of public education, the doctrine of 'separate but equal' has no place."

—Statement from the U.S. Supreme Court decision, *Brown v. Board of Education* May 17, 1954

THURGOOD MARSHALL

Born in Baltimore, Maryland, in 1908, Thurgood Marshall began working for the NAACP in 1934 after studying law at Howard University. Armed with a mastery of legal detail and an in-depth knowledge of the Constitution, Marshall won the nickname "Mr. Civil Rights" for his work in many pioneering legal cases in the 1930s and 1940s. Although *Brown v. Board of Education* was his best known Supreme Court case, Marshall argued 32 cases before the Court, winning all but three of them. In 1961, Marshall moved to the judge's bench when President John F. Kennedy appointed him to the U.S. Court of Appeals. Six years later, President Lyndon Johnson named Marshall the first African-American justice on the Supreme Court. Marshall served on the court until retiring in 1991. He died in 1993.

Thurgood Marshall (center) and his fellow NAACP lawyers George E. C. Hayes (left) and James Nabrit Jr. (right), on the steps of the Supreme Court in Washington, D.C., after their victory in *Brown v. Board of Education. (Library of Congress)*

New York City but not in Atlanta, Georgia, or Mobile, Alabama.

A few advances occurred in the years after World War II. In 1948, President Truman ordered the integration of the U.S. armed forces. The following year, Congress passed a law banning discrimination in hiring for federal jobs.

Many white southern politicians, however, fought all attempts by the federal government to protect civil rights for African Americans. While many white lawmakers were openly racist, they also opposed integration on the basis of the principle of states' rights—the fact that the Constitution gives to the individual states the powers that are not specifically granted to the federal government.

Children study in a segregated grammar school classroom in the 1950s. In the South, educational segregation was a matter of law, but many school systems in the rest of the country were segregated by custom. *(Library of Congress)*

Defenders of segregation also pointed to *Plessy v. Ferguson,* the 1896 Supreme Court ruling that made segregation legal in the first place. In *Plessy,* the court ruled that the Constitution allows the separation of races in schools, hospitals, trains, and other facilities as long as facilities for whites and African Americans are "separate but equal." In practice, facilities for African Americans were almost always inferior to those for whites. From 1938 on, the nation's largest civil-rights organization, the National Association for the Advancement of Colored People (NAACP), challenged *Plessy* in various courts.

The case that finally brought down *Plessy* had its origins not in the South but in Topeka, Kansas. Oliver Brown was a black man who lived in a mostly white neighborhood in that city. He was angry that his daughter Linda had to take a long walk through a

CHARGE IT

In the 1950s, Americans got a new way to pay for all the products they saw advertised on television—the credit card. Its inventor was New York banker Frank McNamara, and the inspiration for the card came when he found he did not have enough cash to pay a restaurant bill one night in 1950. McNamara decided to set up a system called the Diners Club, in which people could pay for meals with a card instead of cash; his company would pay the restaurant owners while charging users of the Diners Club card the cost of their meals and a fee. Soon other companies, including American Express, began issuing cards that let consumers buy now and pay later.

An early Diners Club credit card was advertised with the slogan, "Why should people be limited to spending what they are carrying in cash, instead of being able to spend what they can afford?" written by Diners Club founder Frank McNamara.
(Library of Congress)

railroad yard to get to school everyday, even though there was a school for white children close to her home. In 1951, the local chapter of the NAACP agreed to help Brown challenge the city's segregated school system.

The case made it to the Supreme Court where a brilliant NAACP lawyer, Thurgood Marshall, argued on behalf of Oliver Brown. On May 17, 1954, the justices handed down a unanimous decision in *Brown v. Board of Education of Topeka, Kansas*: School segregation was unconstitutional. In the ruling, the justices stated that the fact that African Americans are not allowed to attend the same schools as white children is proof of inequality. A year later, the Court ordered the nation's school systems to admit African-American and white children equally (a process called integration) "with all deliberate speed."

Although the ruling applied only to public schools, *Brown v. Board of Education* opened the way for challenges to segregation in other areas. It was the first major crack in the wall that separated African Americans from the mainstream of white U.S. society.

THE TELEVISION REVOLUTION

The growing role of television in Americans' lives was one of the biggest developments in the 1950s. The technology behind television was not new. Several scientists, working independently, developed techniques to send pictures and sound across the airwaves in the early 20th century. There were regular television broadcasts in several countries in the 1930s. In the United States, excitement about television began to build in 1939, when the Radio Corporation of America (RCA) televised President Franklin Roosevelt's speech at the opening of the New York World's Fair.

In 1939, however, there were only a few thousand televisions in the entire country. The production of

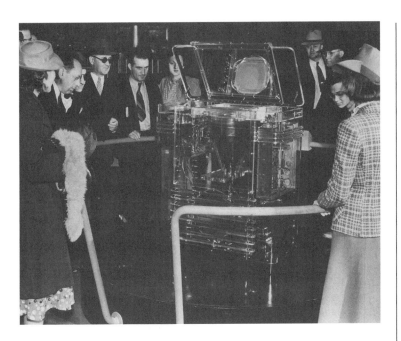

A curious crowd checks out a display model of an early RCA TV, built with a transparent case to show the cathode-ray tube inside. This model was displayed at the 1939 World's Fair, but World War II prevented the mass manufacture and marketing of televisions until the 1950s. *(Library of Congress)*

television sets stopped during World War II because their electronic components were needed for use in radar screens and other military devices needed by the armed forces.

Television production started up again in 1946, but TV, as it began to be called, did not take off right away. The first televisions, which featured three-or-five-inch black-and-white screens, were too expensive for most families. A 1946 RCA television set, for example, cost $350, more than the average U.S. worker made in a month. Also, early television stations had a limited broadcasting range, so most televisions were located in and around major cities where the stations were located.

Throughout the late 1940s, television makers such as RCA, DuMont, Philco, and General Electric began producing more affordable sets. Screen sizes grew to 10 and 12 inches for most sets. Television sales soared. In 1950, 3 million U.S. homes had a television. Just three years later, 25 million homes—half of all the households in the nation—had a television. By the end of the decade, 42 million homes had at least one television, and those sets were turned on for an average of six

THE TV DINNER

Television's influence reached from the living room to the kitchen when the Swanson Frozen Foods Company introduced the TV dinner in 1954. Frozen foods (including Swanson's own pot pies) had been around for years, but the TV dinner marked the first time that a company offered the busy homemaker a complete, frozen individual meal that only had to be heated before serving. The original entrees were roast beef, ham, and fried chicken. Swanson even designed the TV dinner's outer packaging to look like a TV. The family did not have to wait until after dinner to watch TV. Mom could just pop the foil-wrapped meals in the oven. When they were ready, everyone sat down in front of the set and dug in— balancing the meals on little fold-out tables that quickly became known (of course) as TV trays.

"Television is a medium because it is neither rare nor well done."

—Television comic Ernie Kovacs

hours each day. No other technology became such a big part of life so quickly—not even the telephone or the internet.

Television technology advanced rapidly throughout the 1950s. Television stations extended their broadcast ranges using microwave broadcasting and, in some areas, using cable technology. In 1951, Americans from coast to coast watched the first national television broadcast—a speech by President Truman. In 1954, RCA introduced color television, although less-expensive black-and-white televisions outsold color sets until the 1960s. In 1956, the first videotape recorder came into use. Before then, TV shows had to be either broadcast live or from Kinescope, which filmed images of live broadcasts.

In 1950, there were about 100 television stations in the United States. By the middle of the decade there were more than 500, each associated with one of the three major networks—NBC, CBS, and ABC. (A fourth network, DuMont, went out of business in 1956.) These networks produced programs for local television stations, which were known as the networks' affiliates.

The three major television networks were originally established as radio networks, so radio broadcasting had an important influence on the development of television programs. Many early television shows, in fact, began on the radio. *Meet the Press,* for example, started as a radio show in 1945, moved to television in 1947, and is still a popular news program in the 21st century. The great radio journalist Edward R. Murrow also made the jump to television. Murrow's *See It Now* (1951–58) was the first news program to try to shape people's opinions rather than just reporting on events.

Popular movie styles, such as Westerns, also influenced television programming: *Gunsmoke,* which ran from 1955 to 1975, is a good example. Televised sporting events, especially baseball games and boxing matches, also drew large audiences.

Television also followed radio's system of paying for programs through corporate sponsorship. In other words, businesses paid the networks to tie their brand names to particular shows. For example, General Electric sponsored CBS's *General Electric Theater,* which presented plays and musical performances. The show's host was actor and future president Ronald Reagan. At that time, a corporation paid about $1 million to sponsor a show for the usual season of 39 weekly episodes.

Besides corporate sponsorship, television stations paid for programming by selling advertising time to businesses. Most shows broke for a couple of minutes' worth of commercials every 15 minutes or so.

A typical TV broadcast day began with news in the morning, followed by the romantic dramas known as soap operas, because their advertisers were often soap companies. Before and after school hours, there were children's shows such as *Puppet Time Theater* (better known as *The Howdy Doody Show*), *Captain Kangaroo,* and Walt Disney's *The Mickey Mouse Club.* After dinner, families often gathered in the living room to watch television together, so the networks broadcast their most popular shows during the early evening. Because this after-dinner time slot drew the largest number of viewers, it became known as "prime time"—the best time for advertisers to reach a big audience.

Situation comedies, usually centered on a family or group of people in a community, soon became a television mainstay. The most popular situation comedy of the 1950s, by far, was *I Love Lucy,* starring the real-life married couple of Desi Arnaz and Lucille Ball. In 1952, *I Love Lucy* became the first television show to attract an audience of more than 10 million viewers for a single episode. Soon these humorous programs became known as sitcoms.

Variety shows, which featured comedians, musicians, and other performers and celebrities, were another prime-time staple. *Texaco Star Theater,* which ran from

A suburban housewife appears thrilled to have a TV in the kitchen in this advertisement. *(Library of Congress)*

Host Buffalo Bob Smith poses with Clarabell the Clown and Howdy Doody, the marionette star of the hugely popular kids' show *Puppet Time Theater.* *(Library of Congress)*

The CBS network pioneered TV news with a roster of broadcasters that included (from left to right) Eric Sevareid, Edward R. Murrow, Walter Cronkite, and Lowell Thomas. All had distinguished careers as print journalists and radio broadcasters before moving to television. *(Library of Congress)*

The antics of a chimpanzee named J. Fred Muggs livened up NBC's *Today Show,* which Dave Garroway hosted from 1952 to 1961. *(Library of Congress)*

1948 to 1953, was so popular that its host, comedian Milton Berle, won the nickname Mr. Television. On Sunday nights from 1948 to 1971, former radio star Ed Sullivan hosted *Toast of the Town* (later renamed *The Ed Sullivan Show*). Sullivan helped launch the careers of many major entertainers, including Elvis Presley and the Beatles in the 1960s.

After the late evening news, most television stations shut down: Twenty-four hour TV programming was still in the future. In 1954, however, NBC introduced the first late-night talk show, *Tonight!* (later changed to *The Tonight Show*), hosted by Steve Allen. Jack Paar took over hosting duties in 1957. The first daytime talk show, *The Today Show,* began broadcasting in 1952, with Dave Garroway as host.

Television soon began to have an impact on U.S. politics, as events such as presidential speeches and nominating conventions hit the airwaves. The televised Senate hearings investigating Joseph McCarthy's charges against the U.S. Army, for example, played a major role in the senator's downfall and eventual censure by the Senate.

As television grew in popularity, some people questioned whether the new technology's influence was all good. One university president had claimed that television would create "a nation of morons" as people spent more time staring at the television screen and less time reading or talking. One nickname for the television was "idiot box."

Television's influence on children also caused much concern among adults. By the end of the decade, many children spent as much time in front of the television set as they did in the classroom. Some critics accused parents

The RCA CT-100 was the first commercial color television set made in the United States. It cost $1,000—the equivalent of about $7,000 dollars in 2005. *(Library of Congress)*

"We love Lucy too so we're closing on Monday nights."

—Sign in a Chicago department store window

Many episodes of *I Love Lucy* centered on Lucy's attempts to "get into the act" of her bandleader husband, Ricky. *(Library of Congress)*

Rod Serling's well-crafted tales of both supernatural and psychological terror made *The Twilight Zone* one of the most innovative programs of the late 1950s. *(Library of Congress)*

The clean-cut Cleaver family of *Leave it to Beaver,* which ran from 1957 to 1963, first on CBS and then on ABC, was typical of the wholesome, small-town version of American life presented by TV in the 1950s. *(Library of Congress)*

of letting television become an electronic babysitter. Most children's programs in the 1950s were meant to entertain rather than educate. Some stations experimented with educational programs in the 1950s, but the idea that television should help children and adults learn did not become widely accepted until the creation of the Public Broadcasting System (PBS) in the 1960s.

The Americans shown on the television screen were also very different from real Americans. The families in shows such as *Father Knows Best* and *Leave It to Beaver* never seemed to have any serious problems: Mom always had dinner on the table when Dad came home from work, and the kids were always polite. If there were any problems, they were minor ones, and they were always solved by the end of each half-hour episode—usually after some wise advice from Dad.

Few shows included characters who were African American, Hispanic American, or Asian American. The shows that did include African Americans, such as *Amos 'n' Andy,* usually portrayed them in a way that would be considered racist in the 21st century. American Indians were rarely seen on TV except as hostile Indians in Westerns.

In any case, the television revolution of the 1950s included some important cultural achievements. In 1951, for example, NBC broadcast the first opera composed for television—Gian Carlo Menotti's *Amahl and the Night Visitors.* Several writers created brilliant teleplays for live broadcast on shows such as Playhouse 90, including Paddy Chayefsky's *Marty* (1953), Gore Vidal's *Visit to a Small Planet* (1955), and Rod Serling's *Requiem for a Heavyweight* (1956). Serling also created the eerie but intelligent science-fiction series *The Twilight Zone* (1959–64).

CHAPTER 4

NONVIOLENCE AND CONFORMITY, 1954–1956

W HEN THE REPUBLICANS BECAME the majority party in Congress after the election of 1952, it seemed likely that Republican senator Joseph McCarthy would become an even more powerful figure. The head of the Senate Permanent Investigating Committee, McCarthy began investigating accused Communists in the government and the military.

"Is that steak done yet, Daddy?" A suburban family enjoys a backyard barbecue. *(Library of Congress)*

> *"Have you no sense of decency, sir? At long last, have you no sense of decency?"*
>
> —Lawyer Joseph Welch to Senator Joseph McCarthy during the Army-McCarthy hearings, 1954

However, many Americans had come to realize that McCarthy's investigations were not turning up many actual communists. McCarthy's fellow Republicans also became worried when McCarthy attacked respected military officers. Although President Eisenhower disliked McCarthy and his methods, the president refused to speak out against them, believing that it would dishonor the office of the presidency to get into a public clash with the senator.

In late 1953, one of McCarthy's assistants, G. David Schine, was drafted into the U.S. Army. McCarthy accused the army of deliberately hampering his investigations. The army then revealed that McCarthy had used his power to try to get special treatment for Schine.

The result was a dramatic series of special Senate hearings in the summer of 1954. For 36 days, tens of millions of Americans watched as McCarthy and his staff argued with army lawyers. In these hearings, McCarthy appeared to many Americans to be a rude, reckless bully rather than a gallant fighter against communism.

The Democrats won a majority in Congress in the 1954 midterm elections, and, as a result, McCarthy lost the leadership of his committee. A few weeks later, the Senate voted 66 to 22 to censure McCarthy. This action meant that the majority of senators officially disapproved of McCarthy's actions, which had brought the Senate "into dishonor and disrepute."

Powerless and disgraced, McCarthy quickly faded from the scene and died in 1957. His fall from power ended an ugly chapter in U.S. history.

THE MONTGOMERY BUS BOYCOTT

Brown v. Board of Education was a big victory for the civil rights movement, but it applied only to segregation in education. Segregation laws—often called "Jim Crow" laws after an old song—were still on the books in most communities in the South in the mid-1950s.

One such community was Montgomery, Alabama, a city so segregated that a local law forbade African Americans and Whites from playing cards together. On December 1, 1955, Rosa Parks, an African-American clothing worker, boarded a city bus. Tired after a long day of work, Parks sat down in the "Whites Only" section at the front of the bus. When the driver demanded that she move to the back of the bus, Parks refused. The police came and took Parks to jail.

Montgomery's African-American community responded by organizing a one-day boycott of the city's bus system. Because most of Montgomery's African-American citizens were too poor to own cars, they made up 80 percent of the bus company's customers. The boycott's organizers hoped that if African

Bus travel was segregated in the southern states, with separate seating on the bus, separate bathroom facilities and water fountains, and even separate waiting rooms. *(AP/Wide World)*

Martin Luther King Jr. speaks to reporters during the Montgomery bus boycott. King later received the Nobel Peace Prize for his civil rights leadership. *(AP/Wide World)*

"Nonviolence is the most potent technique for oppressed peoples."

—Martin Luther King Jr., 1956

Americans stayed off the buses, the bus company would lose so much money that it would agree to change its rules. The boycott was a hardship for the African-American community, even though the city's African-American taxi drivers promised to transport people for the same 10-cent fare as the bus.

The boycott's organizers included the ministers of Montgomery's African-American churches. One of them was 26-year-old Martin Luther King Jr., newly arrived in town as pastor of the Dexter Avenue Baptist Church.

While studying for the ministry, King had read the writings of the U.S. writer and philosopher Henry David Thoreau and the Indian leader Mohandas Gandhi. In the 19th century, Thoreau went to jail rather than pay a tax to the U.S. government to support its war with Mexico, a conflict he thought was wrong. In the 20th century, Gandhi used boycotts and hunger strikes to help advance the movement to free India from British rule.

Both Thoreau and Gandhi believed that the way to change society was through nonviolent protest. Beginning in the twentieth century, this technique has also been called passive resistance. In their view, people should disobey unjust laws and accept the consequences, even if the consequences include arrests, jail time, or police beatings. Only through peaceful means—by loving one's enemies—can people truly change their enemies' hearts and achieve lasting justice.

These ideas deeply influenced King, and he saw the bus boycott as a way to put them to work in the battle against segregation. A brilliant speaker with a forceful personality, King quickly became the leader of the

EMMETT TILL

One of the worst episodes of racial hatred and violence in the 1950s took place in the small town of Money, Mississippi, in August 1955. Emmett Till, a 14-year-old African American from Chicago, came to Mississippi to spend the summer with relatives. On August 25, Till and some friends were hanging out at a local store. No one knows exactly what happened next, but Till may have bragged that he had a white girlfriend in Chicago, or he may have whistled at the young white woman who ran the store. When the woman's husband heard about the comment from his wife, he and his half-brother kidnapped Till, shot him, and dropped his body in a river, where it was found three days later. Although there was clear evidence of the brothers' guilt, an all-white jury quickly acquitted the men accused of the murder.

The Justice Department reopened the case in May 2004 and exumed Till's body in June 2005.

boycott movement. He declared that the bus boycott would not be for only one day—it would end when Montgomery integrated its entire bus system.

The boycott lasted more than a year. Angry whites firebombed King's house while his wife and baby daughter were inside; they narrowly escaped death and injury. King and other boycott leaders were jailed for a time. Yet King and the boycotters neither backed down from their nonviolent protest nor gave in to the urge to strike back. "So many people have been taught to hate, taught from the cradle. They are not totally responsible," King said of the whites who were using every means, legal and illegal, to break the boycott.

In November 1956, the U.S. Supreme Court ruled that segregation on buses was unconstitutional. On December 21, the boycott ended when Montgomery's city government agreed to obey the Court's decision.

Brown v. Board of Education cracked the wall of segregation. The wall started to crumble after the Montgomery Bus Boycott. The success of the boycott also won national fame for King and established him as one of the civil rights movement's most influential leaders.

"What's good for General Motors is good for the rest of America."

—GM chairman
Charles Wilson, 1955

A few of the nearly 60 million cars bought by Americans in the 1950s zip down a newly constructed freeway. The expansion of the nation's road network knitted suburbs and cities together and made Americans even more dependent on the automobile for transportation. *(Library of Congress)*

CHANGING WAYS OF U.S. LIFE

The movement to the suburbs, which began when the veterans came home from World War II, continued into the 1950s. Between 1950 and 1955, for example, the population growth rate of the nation's suburbs was seven times that of its cities. Suburbanization changed the U.S. landscape and led to a new way of life for tens of millions of people.

There were several reasons for the growth of the suburbs. First, the United States still had plenty of open land close to its major cities. Real-estate developers such as William Levitt, who built Levittown on Long Island in the late 1940s and other Levittowns in Pennsylvania in the early 1950s, were quick to buy farmland and build developments of inexpensive houses. During the 1950s, more than three-quarters of the 15 million new homes in the United States were constructed in the suburbs.

Second, more people could now afford to buy homes of their own. Because of the G.I. Bill, the federal government guaranteed home loans to millions of veterans. The thriving economy meant bigger paychecks for many workers, making the dream of home ownership a reality for people earning even a modest

salary. Just over half of U.S. families owned their own homes in 1950. By 1960, almost two-thirds did.

Third, affordable cars and cheap gas helped make the suburban lifestyle possible. So did the boom in road and highway construction, which made it convenient to drive to work, to shopping, and to leisure activities.

But the biggest reason for the movement to the suburbs was because people saw them as a good place to bring up kids—and there were lots of kids. In the troubled, uncertain years of the Great Depression and World War II in the 1930s and 1940s, Americans often married later in life and had relatively fewer children. Starting in the late 1940s, however, Americans began marrying younger and the size of the average family grew. Some polls in the late 1940s showed that a majority of newlywed couples wanted to have families of four or even more children.

For these young families, the suburbs provided homes with lots of space and backyards for children to play in, as well as good schools and safe streets. With so many people of the same age group living in suburban neighborhoods, the suburbs also offered families a sense of a shared way of life with their neighbors.

In earlier decades, when housing was more expensive, Americans often lived with their extended families, with parents, children, grandparents, and other relatives living under the same roof. In the 1950s, many young families could afford a home of their own. As a result, the so-called nuclear family became more common, in which only two parents and their children shared a home. With the eight-hour workday and the five-day work week standard for many Americans, families also had more time to spend together.

THE COMFORTS OF THE SUBURBAN HOME

In most suburban developments, the houses were built in a few standard styles. Some houses were constructed

A typical suburban ranch house of the 1950s came complete with attached garage and attic space for expansion as the family grew. *(Library of Congress)*

in the so-called Cape Cod or Colonial styles and were based on earlier American house designs. The most common house style of the 1950s was the one-story ranch house. Another popular style was the split-level or raised ranch, which allowed more living space on a small lot.

In earlier times, most houses contained a lot of small rooms, including a parlor and a dining room for entertaining. The new suburban houses featured more open living spaces that flowed into one another—a style that grew out of the ideas of 20th-century architect Frank Lloyd Wright. Many suburban houses were also built with unfinished basements and attics, allowing homeowners to add more rooms as their families grew. Many suburban houses had a garage or carport for the family car, a front lawn, and a backyard, often with a patio or deck.

The interior of the suburban house reflected a new, more casual lifestyle. With fewer people living in each house, families often ate their meals in the kitchen, reserving the dining room for formal occasions. Family life centered on the living room, where everyone often gathered after dinner to watch television. Wood-paneled basements became family rooms or playrooms for children and teens. Outdoor gatherings, especially backyard barbecues, became popular weekend and holiday activities.

Suburban homes also featured a variety of appliances. Electric appliances had been around since the 1920s, but only after World War II did they become inexpensive enough for many families to afford them. Electric washers and dryers replaced washtubs and clotheslines; electric and gas ranges and ovens replaced coal and wood stoves for cooking; and electric refrigerators replaced iceboxes. Manufacturers produced electric versions of many kitchen tools—mixers, carving knives, coffee pots, and so on.

Prepackaged convenience foods became very popular in U.S. kitchens during the 1950s. Like electrical appliances, convenience foods were supposed to make life easier for homemakers. Frozen foods, including vegetables and TV dinners, were advertised as a way to prepare family meals quickly and easily. Other products, including coffee and other beverages, could be purchased in instant or powdered form by using a technology developed for military rations in World War II.

SUBURBS AND CITIES

Some people felt that suburbanization was not a completely positive development. Critics of the suburbs wondered why people would want to live in neighborhoods where every house looked much like every other house and every street looked much like every other street. These critics charged that the suburbs put pressure on people to conform—to behave like their neighbors, whether they wanted to or not.

Other critics of suburbia noted that the suburbs lack the cultural riches of major cities, such as museums, art galleries, and concert halls. They also pointed out that in cities, people of different races, backgrounds, and social classes mix together, while most suburbanites live among people much the same as themselves.

Suburbanization also led to problems for the nation's major cities. The movement to the suburbs was

Mexican-American children sit outside their school in the 1950s. In the southwestern states, Hispanic Americans endured discrimination and segregation similar to that faced by African Americans. *(Private Collection)*

not the only major population movement of the 1950s. As white, middle-class families moved from the cities to the suburbs, poorer people from nonwhite groups were moving from rural areas to the city.

The Great Migration of African Americans to the cities continued in the 1950s as machinery replaced human labor on the farms and in the textile mills of the South. And although people from Latin America would not immigrate to the United States in large numbers until the 1960s, many Mexicans moved to Los Angeles and other California cities in the 1950s. In addition, people from Puerto Rico, an island in the Caribbean which was a U.S. possession, often moved to New York City in this decade.

Unfortunately, these new city dwellers arrived at a bad time. Earlier waves of immigrants could usually find work, even if it was low-paying, in the many small factories and shops that filled the cities. By the 1950s, however, many of these businesses were in decline, so there were fewer jobs available for the newcomers.

Another serious situation affected city residents. When middle-class families moved to the suburbs, they no longer paid taxes to city governments or spent money in urban shops and stores. As a result, cities started to find it difficult to pay for education and other services for their residents.

The United States was becoming a nation in which suburbs of mainly white, middle-class people surrounded inner cities of poorer people of color. In an effort to solve problems of poverty, unemployment, and crime, many cities turned to what became known as urban renewal. Urban development often meant tearing down old, rundown neighborhoods and replacing them with public housing projects—groups of low-cost, government-funded apartment buildings that housed hundreds and sometimes thousands of people. This housing was supposed to provide a better living environment for poor citizens than the older, overcrowded slums.

In practice, however, city officials found that poverty, crime, and other problems often were worse in the new projects. Some critics charged that the real purpose of urban renewal was to keep the poor away from the wealthy in the cities—a form of urban segregation.

High-rise apartment buildings like the ones shown here were typical of the kind of public housing constructed during the urban-renewal campaigns of the 1950s. *(Library of Congress)*

WOMEN IN THE 1950S

In the 1950s, suburbanization and the nuclear family also had an impact on women in the United States. The 1950s was a decade when there was much pressure on women to look on the role of homemaker as their ideal in life. Finding a husband who would be a good provider was seen as an unmarried woman's goal. Even women who went to college were expected to pay as much attention to finding a husband as getting an education: "Not so long ago," the New York Times newspaper reported in 1954, "girls were expelled from college for marrying; now girls feel hopeless if they have not a marriage at least in sight by [graduation]." Many left without graduating, with a so-called "Mrs." degree.

Gathering for a sewing bee was one of the leisure activities suburban housewives were expected to take part in. *(Library of Congress)*

Thanks to the prosperity of the decade, many families could now afford a middle-class lifestyle on one salary. Earning that salary was the father's role. The mother's role was to make a good home for her husband and children, which meant cooking, cleaning, shopping, and driving the children to Boy Scout or Girl Scout meetings, Little League practice, and music lessons. In her spare time, she might gather with other mothers for coffee or a card game, or she might do volunteer work.

Of course, this kind of life was not the case for all women. Poor women usually had no choice but to work outside the home to add to their husbands' incomes, and they usually had to do the cooking, cleaning, and shopping as well. The wealthy could pay people to do these chores for them, freeing up their time for other activities. But for millions of married women in the suburbs, life revolved around the kitchen and the supermarket, the washing machine, and the children's after-school activities.

Television shows and commercials, magazine and newspaper ads—all promoted the idea that this lifestyle was the kind of life women should want. Many Americans believed that there was something wrong with a woman who wanted a career outside the home, or who wanted to continue her education, or who wanted to delay marriage and children, or who wished not to marry at all.

Being a full-time homemaker could also be exhausting. Electric appliances and convenience foods were supposed to make housework less difficult, but studies showed that many women were spending more time cooking, cleaning, and shopping than their mothers or grandmothers had, in order to meet the standards of a perfect home.

As a result, many women felt frustrated in the 1950s. Women who wanted something else in life besides marriage, motherhood, and homemaking felt guilty because they desired a different kind of life. In a 1957 article in *Life* magazine, for example, several

A family welcomes its newest member—one of the approximately 30 million children born between 1950 and 1960. *(Library of Congress)*

Membership in the Boy and Girl Scouts, Little League, 4H, and other youth organizations rose in the 1950s as the children of the Baby Boom grew up.
(Library of Congress)

psychiatrists claimed that "female ambition" led to mental illness in women and unhappiness for their husbands and children. Even women who were comfortable in their roles as homemakers found it hard to cope with the effort required to live up to the popular image of the good wife and mother.

There were signs of change toward the end of the 1950s. Despite the ideal of the full-time homemaker, the number of women working outside the home rose during the decade. At this time, women workers were usually paid 60 percent less, on average, than men. Women could also look to the examples of successful women such as journalist and diplomat Clare Booth Luce, Senator Margaret Chase Smith, and Secretary of Health, Education, and Welfare Oveta Culp Hobby, a member of President Eisenhower's cabinet from 1953–55. It would not be until the 1960s, however, that the movement for more opportunities for women and equality between men and women, began to gather strength.

THE INTERSTATE HIGHWAY SYSTEM

In 1956, Congress passed the Federal-Aid Highway Act and the Highway Revenue Act. The acts called for the

ROBERT MOSES

No person did more to reshape the city in the image of the car than New York's so-called Master Builder, Robert Moses. Although he was never elected to any office, Moses had enormous power as the head of several city and state agencies. From the 1920s through the 1960s, but especially in the 1950s, Moses used this power to build a huge system of highways, bridges, and tunnels to link New York's suburbs to New York City, which made it easier for cars to travel into and through the city. In the process, his construction projects destroyed entire neighborhoods and used up much of the money that might have gone to improve the city's public transportation system. Moses was also largely responsible for the building of the city's massive, and often troubled, public housing projects. When critics attacked his methods, he replied, "When you operate in an overbuilt metropolis, you have to hack your way with a meat ax."

financing and construction of a huge network of interstate and intercity highways across the United States.

The highway system would serve a defense purpose by allowing the quick movement of troops and equipment in the event of an attack on the United States or some other national emergency. (Overpasses on the new highways, for example, were planned to be high enough to allow trucks carrying long-range missiles to pass underneath.) The system would also benefit the economy by making it easier and faster for people and goods to travel long distances. The highway system had the strong backing of President Eisenhower, as well as the auto industry, which saw that the improved road network would boost car sales even further.

The construction of the interstate highway system was the biggest single public works project in the nation's history. About 7,500 miles of highway were in service by the end of the 1950s. By the time the system was completed in the 1990s, it included more than 42,000 miles. (In 1990, the highway system was officially named the Dwight D. Eisenhower System of Interstate and Defense Highways.)

Oldsmobile's 1955 Holiday 88 sedan weighed almost two tons and featured a four-door hardtop body, a 202-horsepower V-8 engine, an automatic transmission, a two-tone paint job, and a hood ornament that looked like a science-fiction rocketship. *(Library of Congress)*

"The moving van is a symbol of more than our restlessness; it is...evidence of our progress."

—Writer Louis Kronenberger on the movement to the suburbs

The car culture had costs as well as benefits. For example, as more Americans traveled by car and more goods traveled by truck, the nation's once-mighty railroad system fell into a steep decline. In the 1940s, two out of every three Americans traveling from city to city went by train; that number fell to one out of every five by the 1960s. During the same period, the amount of freight carried by railroads dropped from about two-thirds of the total to less than half and the amount of railroad track in use dropped by about 15,000 miles.

The ever-growing number of cars on the road led to an increasing thirst for oil, which is needed to make gasoline. Until around 1953, the United States produced enough oil for its own needs and even exported some oil overseas. After 1953, however, the nation had to import oil to meet its needs.

The kind of cars Americans drove in the 1950s contributed to the need for oil. Because gas was plentiful and cheap, good gas mileage was not a concern for carmakers. In an era before many Americans became concerned about the environment, carmakers did not pay attention to the pollution caused by car exhaust, either. The emphasis was on style, comfort, speed—and especially size. Cars grew bigger, heavier, and flashier

An interchange on one of the new interstate highways. Specifications for the interstate system called for each road to have at least two travel lanes, each of them 12 feet wide. *(Library of Congress)*

every year, with carmakers piling on chrome, tailfins, and other showy touches.

Along with the interstate highway system, another development of the 1950s revolutionized transportation in the United States—jet airliners. At the start of the decade, most passenger aircraft were relatively slow propeller-driven models. While jets were in military service from the mid-1940s on, development of passenger jets lagged behind. Britain and France took an early lead in building passenger jets, but these early aircraft had many problems.

In 1954, the Boeing Company in Washington State introduced the 367-80, a big four-engine jet that was first

THE MALLING OF AMERICA

Many suburbanites had to travel to nearby cities to shop for clothes, furniture, and other goods in the early years of the movement to the suburbs. In 1956, a new era in shopping began in Edina, Minnesota, with the opening of the Southland Center—the nation's first indoor shopping mall. The creation of Austrian-born builder Victor Gruen, Southland grouped 10 acres' worth of stores into a single, fully enclosed, air-conditioned complex, built on two levels connected by escalators. He also added features such as a fishpond, trees, and an enormous cage filled with exotic birds. Suburbanites loved having all the goods they needed under one roof, with plenty of parking. Similar complexes started to pop up across the landscape. Less than 50 years later, there were more than 45,000 malls in the United States, with total sales of more than $1 trillion a year.

used as a flying fuel tanker for the U.S. Air Force. Boeing adapted the design to create the first successful long-range passenger jet, the 707, which could carry up to 179 passengers, at speeds of up to 600 miles per hour.

On October 26, 1958, a Pan American Airways 707 began the first regular jet service between New York and London. Three months later, American Airlines used the 707 to offer nonstop service between New York and Los Angeles. The 707 and competing planes, such as the Douglas DC-8, cut travel time between the East and West coasts and across the Atlantic Ocean almost in half. The jet age had begun.

GROWING UP IN THE 1950s

About 76 million Americans were born between 1946 and 1964, most of them between 1950 and 1960. Never before and never since has such a large number of people grown up at the same time, and shared many of the same experiences and influences. The huge bulge in population is known as the Baby Boom, and those who were born then are often called Baby Boomers.

One influence on the rearing of that generation was a pediatrician named Benjamin Spock. In 1946, Spock published the first edition of his *Common Sense*

Crew cuts and conservative clothes: 1950s teenagers enjoy a snack at an afterschool party. *(Library of Congress)*

A REBEL WITHOUT A CAUSE

Young people who felt restless and misunderstood in the 1950s found a hero in movie actor James Dean, star of *Rebel Without a Cause* (1955). Dean's character, Jim Stark, is a teenager from a good home, but he feels only emptiness and confusion, and he constantly gets into trouble. Jim takes comfort in the company of his girlfriend Judy (played by Natalie Wood) and their friend Plato (played by Sal Mineo), but he faces tragedy when he is unable to stop Plato from being killed in an accidental shooting.

The real-life James Dean was moody and intense, much like the character he played in *Rebel.* Dean did not live to see the movie become a hit. A month before *Rebel* opened in October 1955, he died in a car crash on a California highway at the age of 24. Dean starred in only two movies besides *Rebel* (*East of Eden* and *Giant*), but he lives on in the popular imagination as an actor who captured the spirit of the 1950s.

Left to right are Sal Mineo, James Dean, and Natalie Wood in a scene from *Rebel Without a Cause.* "Teenage terror torn from today's headlines!" proclaimed a poster for the movie. *(Private Collection)*

Book of Baby and Child Care. The book went on to sell more copies than any book other than the Bible and the works of Shakespeare. Millions of new parents relied on Dr. Spock for advice. The book told parents to trust their instincts when it came to raising kids and to be friends with their children. Spock also urged parents to use understanding rather than harsh discipline to encourage their children to behave.

Television was another shared experience of the Baby Boomers, who were the first generation to grow up with television in their homes. Advertisers were quick to realize that commercials aimed at children could sell products in huge numbers. In 1954–55, for example, Walt Disney's *Disneyland* television show ran a popular series about the adventures of Davy Crockett. Sales of raccoon-skin caps—just like the one worn by Fess Parker, the actor who played Crockett—hit 10 million by the end of 1955.

The Baby Boom also led to a boom in education. By the early 1950s, school attendance topped 5 million. The

Actor Fess Parker in costume as Davy Crockett, billed as "King of the Wild Frontier" on his TV show. The price of raccoon skins rose from 2 cents to $5.00 dollars apiece as kids clamored for a cap like the one their hero wore. *(Library of Congress)*

THE GREAT COMIC BOOK CONTROVERSY

Comic books were hugely popular among kids of the 1950s. By the middle of the decade, 20 million 10-cent comics were being sold every month. Many of these comics, such as *Voodoo* and *Uncanny Tales,* featured gory, violent stories about ghosts, zombies, and other monsters. In 1953, psychiatrist Frederic Wertham published a book called *Seduction of the Innocent,* which claimed that comics were damaging children's emotional development and contributing to juvenile delinquency. The book touched off a national controversy. Even Congress got into the act when Senator Estes Kefauver of Tennessee chaired a committee that investigated the influence of comics on children. Under pressure, the leading comic book publishers formed the Comics Code Authority in 1954. They agreed to tone down the gore and violence; the new, cleaned-up comics had a special seal of approval on the cover. A new kind of comic also made its appearance in 1952—*Mad* magazine, which featured spoofs of pop culture.

vast numbers of students put a strain on school systems in many communities. Teachers were in short supply, and many new schools had to be built—more than 15,000 classrooms were created across the country in 1952 alone. Many communities combined smaller schools to make big schools, some with thousands of students.

Not only were more students in school, they were also staying in school longer. In the 1940s, only about half of all Americans graduated from high school. By the end of the 1950s, more than three-quarters received their diplomas.

The rise in high school attendance was part of a growing teenage culture in the 1950s as the children born during World War II and in the first years of the Baby Boom reached their teen years.

For the first time in U.S. history, most young people did not have to leave school to work to help support their families. Many teenagers who worked at part-time jobs were free to spend their earnings on clothes, records (music), perhaps even a used car. For middle-class teens, social life revolved around dates and dances, watching or playing sports, and gathering with friends to listen to music and talk.

If teenagers in the 1950s enjoyed more money and leisure time than teenagers of earlier decades, they also faced a lot of pressure to conform, or to go along with the group. Just as women were expected to want to be homemakers, teenagers were expected to accept the authority of their parents, teachers, and other adults, and to make a good job (if they were boys), marriage, and a family their goals after leaving high school or college. Young people who questioned authority, or who did not want this kind of lifestyle, often felt lonely and troubled.

Yet many people who grew up in the 1950s remember the decade as a happy time. Worries about the cold war were always in the background, but after the Korean War ended, the nation was at peace. Unlike their parents and grandparents, the Baby Boomers did not experience the poverty of the Great Depression or the uncertainty of World War II. The children of the growing suburban middle class enjoyed a higher standard of living than ever before, at a time when the United States seemed sure of its role in the world.

There were some troubling trends among the nation's young people, however. One was the growing number of crimes committed by teenagers. In the mid-1950s, for example, studies showed that criminals under the age of 21 committed half of all the robberies in some of the nation's major cities. A book published in 1956 used the term *juvenile delinquency* to describe this development.

There was much debate about what caused young people to become juvenile delinquents. Some people blamed busy parents who were not closely involved with their children. Other Americans thought that children of divorced parents were more likely to turn to crime. And some experts blamed the influence of comic books and movies on young people.

A young married couple is portrayed at home. By 1959, the average age at marriage for American women was 19. *(Library of Congress)*

HAIL! HAIL! ROCK 'N' ROLL

In the early 1950s, smooth-sounding singers, such as Rosemary Clooney, Nat King Cole, Teresa Brewer, and Mario Lanza dominated U.S. popular music. Outside of the mainstream of pop music, however, other styles

"Awopbobaloobop—alopbamboom! Tutti-frutti! All rootie!"

—Opening of Little Richard's hit song "Tutti Frutti," 1955

THE MAGIC KINGDOM

In July 1954, workers began to transform a 160-acre orange grove in the Los Angeles suburb of Anaheim, California, into the world's first theme park. Disneyland was the brainchild of moviemaker Walt Disney. His vision called for a family-friendly park filled with rides and other attractions inspired by his movies and by his vision of the past, present, and future of the United States. For example, he designed the park to include places such as Main Street, USA, which recalls the main street of a typical U.S. town at the turn of the 20th century; Frontierland, which celebrates the Old West of the 19th century; and Tomorrowland, which gives visitors a look at designers' ideas of the marvels of the future. Construction began just a year before the park was scheduled to open. On opening day—July 17, 1955—28,000 people streamed through the gates, far more than the park had room for at the time. Rides broke down, restaurants ran out of food and drink, and it was so hot that people's shoes got stuck in the melting asphalt on Main Street, USA. Once the park's problems were worked out, Disneyland was a huge success, with more than 50 million visitors in its first 10 years. The Walt Disney Company later built Disney World, an even bigger theme park in Florida, as well as parks in Japan and Europe.

were beginning to blend together to form a new, exciting kind of music that would take the nation's young people by storm.

One such style of music was rhythm and blues, or R&B. As African Americans moved to the cities, they brought the blues music of the rural South with them. Traditional blues singers usually accompanied themselves on an acoustic guitar, but it was hard to hear this instrument in the crowded, noisy nightclubs of city neighborhoods such as Chicago's South Side. In the 1940s, guitarists, such as Howlin' Wolf, Muddy Waters, and John Lee Hooker, switched to electric guitars and added drums, bass guitar, piano, and other instruments to their bands. They also sped up the blues tempo to make a distinct sound.

Another style was country music, sometimes called country & western. This was a modern version of the folk music of white settlers in the South and Southwest. Country music began to build a national audience in the 1920s, but it made a big leap in popularity after 1949, when Hank Williams's song "Lovesick Blues," a number one hit on the country charts, crossed over to be included in the Top 20 songs on the national pop music charts.

During the early 1950s, R&B and country music started to blend. Performers began to play songs with the driving beat of R&B and the bright guitar sound of country music. This new music mixed in elements of gospel music and other styles, too. In 1954, a Cleveland disc jockey (DJ) named Alan Freed gave the new style its name—rock 'n' roll.

African-American artists released songs in a rock 'n' roll style in the early 1950s, but it was a group of white musicians, Bill Haley and His Comets, which scored the first big rock 'n' roll hit with "Rock around the Clock." The song was released in 1954, but it was not until a year later, when the song was used in the soundtrack of the hit movie Blackboard Jungle, that it shot to number one on the pop charts.

Over the next couple of years a remarkable group of rock 'n' roll performers, both white and African-American, hit the scene. From St. Louis, Missouri, came African-American singer and guitarist Chuck Berry, who did much to define the new rock 'n' roll style with songs such as "Maybellene," "Rock and Roll Music," and "Johnny B. Goode." From Macon, Georgia, came African-American Richard Penniman, better known as Little Richard, who became famous for his stage antics, such as playing the piano with his feet. From Louisiana came the white performer Jerry Lee Lewis, another wild piano-pounder. From Lubbock, Texas, came white musician Buddy Holly, whose band, the Crickets, was the first real rock group.

The performer who really made rock 'n' roll famous was a young white truck driver from Memphis, Tennessee, named Elvis Presley. In 1953, Presley walked into Sun Records in Memphis and paid four dollars to make a record as a present for his mother. When Sam Phillips, Sun's owner, heard Elvis's voice, he decided he had a star on his hands.

Phillips teamed Presley with bassist Bill Black and guitarist Scotty Moore and started recording. Philips was

Chuck Berry does his trademark duck walk in this scene from *Hail! Hail! Rock 'n' Roll,* a movie celebrating Berry's music. *(Library of Congress)*

"Rock and roll music, if you like it, if you feel it, you can't help but move to it," Elvis, shown in a recording studio, told an interviewer. "That's what happens to me. I can't help it." *(Library of Congress)*

*"He can't last.
I tell you flatly,
he can't last."*

—Comedian Jackie Gleason
on Elvis Presley, 1956

not happy with the results until the trio struck up an R&B song, "That's Alright Mama," originally recorded by the African-American singer Arthur "Big Boy" Crudup. Presley's version was released in 1954. Elvis's career really took off in 1956–57 when he released a string of huge hits, which included "Heartbreak Hotel," "Hound Dog," "Don't Be Cruel," and "All Shook Up."

As a performer, Presley created a sensation everywhere he played. Wearing tight jeans or flashy suits, he swiveled his hips and thrashed around onstage with a wild energy that had never been seen before in popular music. (His hip-swiveling style gave rise to his nickname, Elvis the Pelvis.) When he appeared on *The Ed Sullivan Show* in September 1956, 60 million people tuned in—the largest television audience up to that time.

Young people loved rock 'n' roll. By the late 1950s teenagers were buying almost three-quarters of all the records sold in the United States. Gathering at a diner or soda shop to listen to records on the jukebox became an after-school ritual for millions of teenagers, as did watching Dick Clark's *American Bandstand* television show, in which a studio audience danced and rated the latest hits.

Many teenagers' parents and other older and more conservative Americans hated the new music. Some charged that rock 'n' roll contributed to the growing problem of juvenile delinquency. A number of religious groups claimed rock 'n' roll's rhythms lured teenagers into immorality. It was for this reason that the television cameras broadcast Elvis the Pelvis only from the waist up when he first appeared on *The Ed Sullivan Show.*

There was a strong element of racism in the protest against rock 'n' roll, especially in the South. The fact that many rock 'n' roll performers were African American angered many whites. Southern white adults were also disturbed that African-American and white teenagers mixed freely at rock 'n' roll concerts and dances.

CHAPTER 5

LITTLE ROCK TO *SPUTNIK,* 1956–1958

PRESIDENT EISENHOWER SOUGHT A second term in 1956. His age and health were issues during the campaign. The president was now 66 years old. He had suffered a heart attack in 1955 and was operated on for a stomach condition the following year. Eisenhower bounced back quickly from both illnesses, however, and he easily won the Republican nomination. Once again, the Democrats chose Adlai Stevenson as their candidate, and Senator Estes Kefauver was selected as his running mate.

The conflict between the state of Arkansas and the federal government over the integration of Little Rock's Central High School was one the major domestic issues of President Eisenhower's second term. *(Library of Congress)*

Eisenhower won by a landslide, defeating Stevenson by almost 10 million votes. The Democrats, however, gained a majority in both the Senate and the House of Representatives, and they added more seats to their gains in the midterm elections of 1958. For the first time in more than a century, one party was in the White House without holding a majority in either house of Congress.

THE LITTLE ROCK CRISIS

As the movement for civil rights for African Americans gathered strength, so did opposition from many southern whites. Despite the Supreme Court's order that schools must integrate "with all deliberate speed," many communities refused to do so, with the backing of their state governments. In towns and cities throughout the South, segregationists and white supremacists (people who believed that the white race was superior to all others) formed groups called White Citizens' Councils to fight school integration and to prevent African Americans from voting.

There were many ways in which African Americans were denied the vote. In some southern states, voters had to pay a poll tax, which many poor African Americans could not afford. In other states, passing a literacy test was a requirement for voting, but the test questions were usually rigged so that any white could pass but most African Americans were likely to fail.

In many places, racist groups, such as the Ku Klux Klan, kept African Americans from registering to vote or voting by using violence and terror. In 1955, a 63-year-old African-American World War II veteran was shot to death in Brookhaven, Mississippi, while calling for the right to vote. Although there were many witnesses to the murder, no one was ever convicted. This case was just one of many such incidents throughout the South.

White supremacists also used less violent but equally damaging methods to keep African Americans from their rights. African Americans who tried to register for the vote or integrate local schools often found their names printed in local newspapers. Many white employers then fired them, and banks with white ownership refused to loan them money or let them use credit.

In August 1957, Congress took a step toward guaranteeing the rights of all Americans to vote, regardless of their race or their state of residence, by passing the Civil Rights Act of 1957. The first federal civil rights law since 1875, the act made the U.S. Department of Justice responsible for the protection of citizens' right to vote and other civil liberties, including the right to sit on a jury. With the passage of this new law, African Americans who were denied the right to vote in their home states had their cases tried in federal court instead of a state court, which had ruled unfavorably in years past.

The Civil Rights Act of 1957 was a step forward, but not a big enough step. It gave the Justice Department responsibility but not much authority. The Justice Department found it hard to get southern officials to obey federal court decisions or to punish them when they kept African Americans from the polls. To strengthen the law, a second civil rights act was passed in 1960. This law called for fines or prison sentences for anyone found guilty of denying voting rights.

The conflict over school integration became a crisis in September 1957 when Arkansas governor Orval Faubus refused to allow the integration of Central High School in Little Rock, the state capital. Faubus called out troops of the Arkansas National Guard to keep nine African-American students from registering for classes.

Faubus's action put President Eisenhower in a difficult position. Eisenhower did not believe that the federal government should take the lead in advancing civil

On orders from Governor Orval Faubus, Arkansas National Guard troops bar African-American students—soon dubbed the Little Rock Nine in the press—from entering Central High. *(Library of Congress)*

"Mob rule cannot be allowed to override the decisions of our courts."

—President Eisenhower during the Little Rock crisis

rights. Yet Faubus challenged the authority of the federal government by refusing to obey the Supreme Court's decision in *Brown v. Board of Education.*

Under pressure from Eisenhower, Faubus backed down and called off the National Guard troops, but the crisis continued. When the African-American students entered the school on September 23, an angry mob of more than1,000 whites surrounded the school. The Little Rock Nine, as the African-American students were called, had to leave the school for their own safety.

The president acted swiftly, sending 1,000 U.S. Army troops to Little Rock. He also ordered 10,000 troops of the Arkansas National Guard into federal service. Under the protection of all of these soldiers, four of the Little Rock Nine returned to Central High on September 25. The troops remained in Little Rock for two months.

The Little Rock crisis helped change public opinion about integration. Many Americans in all parts of the country were shamed by televised images of angry whites threatening to attack young students. Americans were also disturbed that troops had to be used to enforce the law. After Little Rock, more and more people questioned how the United States—a nation dedicated to promoting freedom around the world—could permit such scenes at home.

A crowd of whites taunts Elizabeth Eckford, one of the Little Rock Nine, after she was denied entry to Central High on September 4, 1957. *(Library of Congress)*

The Civil Rights Act of 1957 and the Little Rock crisis also showed that the federal government would act in defense of civil rights. For many Americans, white and black, it was not enough. In the late 1950s several new civil rights groups formed, not only to urge the government to move forward on civil rights, but also to fight for equality in all areas of U.S. society.

These groups included the Southern Christian Leadership Conference (SCLC), founded by Martin Luther King Jr. in 1957, the Congress of Racial Equality (CORE), and the Student Nonviolent Coordinating Committee (SNCC). Their members worked throughout the South, registering African Americans to vote, educating them about their rights, and setting up local branches of these organizations.

At the end of the decade, the civil rights movement added a new form of nonviolent resistance to segregation—the sit-in. In 1960, college students in Greensboro, North Carolina, sat down at a lunch counter in a segregated department store and refused to leave. Soon, similar sit-ins took place in bus stations, restaurants, stores, movie theaters, and other segregated facilities throughout the South.

"The Law cannot change the heart—but it can restrain the heartless," said Martin Luther King Jr., the first president of the Southern Christian Leadership Conference (SCLC). *(Library of Congress)*

The civil rights movement had come far in the six years since *Brown v. Board of Education.* It had grown out of small local protests into a mass movement that now attracted support from many Americans of all races. But the movement faced determined resistance. Long years of even greater struggle remained ahead for those who demanded that the United States live up to the Constitution's Bill of Rights, which guarantees freedom and justice to all Americans.

THE UNITED STATES AND THE DEVELOPING WORLD

Before World War II, large parts of Asia, Africa, and the Middle East were ruled by European powers, including Britain and France. In the years after the war, however, increasing numbers of people around the world demanded independence from European rule. India, which was ruled by Britain until 1947, gained independence without war. Other colonies, such as those controlled by the French in Indochina and North Africa, won freedom only after bitter warfare.

This growing spirit of nationalism around the world put the United States in an awkward position. On the one hand, the United States supported the right of people to decide their own form of government. On the other hand, the United States was committed to halting the spread of communism, and many nationalist movements were politically Communist. The U.S. leaders believed that no Communist nation could be truly free, because it would be subject to the influence of China or the Soviet Union. For this reason, the United States supported the French colonists in Indochina.

Egyptian leader Gamel Abdel Nasser's seizure of the Suez Canal in July 1956 sparked an international crisis that strained relations between the United States and three of its allies: Britain, France, and Israel. *(Library of Congress)*

Aside from the issue of communism, the United States had to deal with practical considerations in its relations with the rest of the world. In the 1950s, the economies of the United States and its allies were growing more and more dependent on imported oil. Much of this oil came from the Middle East. Safeguarding the flow of oil from the Middle East and resistance to Soviet influence in the region became the priorities of the Eisenhower administration. The situation in the Middle East was complicated by the fact that the United States supported the Jewish nation of Israel while the Arab nations of the region, such as Egypt, Syria, and Jordan, were bitterly opposed to Israel's existence.

The first major test of U.S. Middle Eastern policy came during the Suez Crisis of 1956. The crisis was sparked by the actions of Gamel Abdel Nasser, Egypt's ruler. Nasser wanted to develop Egypt's economy by building a huge dam on the Nile River. The United States

Connecting the Mediterranean Sea with the Indian Ocean, the Suez Canal, shown here, was an important waterway for international trade. *(Library of Congress)*

and Britain offered loans to Egypt to help build the dam. When the United States learned that Nasser had also asked the Soviet Union for aid, the United States and Britain refused to loan any money.

Nasser responded by seizing the Suez Canal—an Egyptian waterway that connected the Mediterranean Sea to the Indian Ocean, and which was vital to world trade. Nasser also stepped up Egyptian attacks on Israel.

While U.S. diplomats tried to resolve the crisis, France, Britain, and Israel decided to act on their own. In October, while Eisenhower was campaigning for reelection, Israel invaded Egypt with help from British and French forces.

This action angered Eisenhower. While he was opposed to Nasser's seizure of the canal and the attacks on Israel, he believed that Britain, France, and Israel were making the situation worse. Secretary of State John Foster Dulles asked the United Nations to pass a resolution calling for the withdrawal of foreign troops from Egypt. The Soviet Union supported the resolution—a rare example of U.S.-Soviet cooperation during the cold war. Under pressure from Eisenhower and the

Although his books were usually set in an imaginary future, author Ray Bradbury's science fiction commented on concerns of the 1950s, including racism and the danger of nuclear war. *(Library of Congress)*

SCIENCE FACT AND SCIENCE FICTION

Advances in science and the start of the space age fueled a boom in science fiction during the 1950s. Movies such as *The Thing* (1951), *It Came From Outer Space* (1953), and *Invasion of the Body Snatchers* (1956) portrayed humans in conflict with alien life forms. One of the best science-fiction movies of the decade, *The Day the Earth Stood Still* (1951), suggested that because of nuclear weapons, humankind's worst enemy was now itself. The decade also saw the publication of several science-fiction novels that became classics, including Isaac Asimov's *Foundation Trilogy,* Ray Bradbury's *The Martian Chronicles* and *Fahrenheit 451,* Robert Heinlein's *Starship Troopers,* and Kurt Vonnegut's *The Sirens of Titan.* There were also more than 30 science-fiction television series in the 1950s; the most popular was probably *Captain Video,* which ran on the DuMont network from 1949 until the network went out of business in 1954.

United Nations, the British, French, and Israelis withdrew.

SCIENCE, SPACE, AND SPUTNIK

Fear of a nuclear war was never far from Americans' minds in the 1950s. Despite the thaw in the cold war that began after Joseph Stalin's death in 1953, the world's two super-powers—the United States and the Soviet Union—remained at odds. The Soviet Union's new leader, Nikita Khrushchev, believed that Soviet-style communism would eventually triumph throughout the world. In November 1956 Khrushchev told a group of U.S. and European diplomats, "Whether you like it or not, history is on our side. We will bury you."

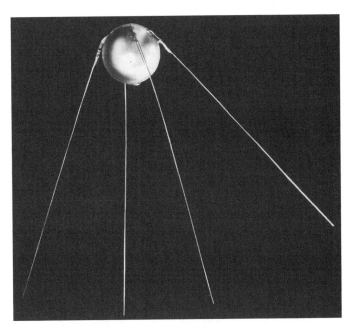

Sputnik 1 (shown here) was about the size of a basketball. A month later, the Soviets launched a much larger satellite, *Sputnik 2,* with a dog named Laika aboard. American reporters nicknamed the dog "muttnik." *(Library of Congress)*

To counter the threat of a Soviet attack, the United States developed more powerful nuclear weapons throughout the 1950s. In May 1952, the U.S. Atomic Energy Commission exploded the world's first hydrogen bomb, or H-bomb, on the Pacific island of Eniwetok.

The new weapon made earlier atomic bombs look like firecrackers. The H-bomb had the explosive power of a million tons of non-nuclear explosives. This amount was more than three times the explosive energy of all the explosives used by all nations in World War II. In addition, when the new bombs were tested, they released huge amounts of deadly radiation that could poison the earth for many decades.

Not long after the United States tested the H-bomb, the Soviets exploded an H-bomb of their own. It was now clear that a nuclear war would probably kill millions of people and possibly wipe out life on Earth. It was also evident that there could be no real winner in a nuclear war

"Maybe the Russians will steal all our secrets. Then they'll be two years behind."

—Comedian Mort Sahl after the *Sputnik* launch

A mushroom cloud rises over the site of the first hydrogen-bomb test. The H-bomb used an atomic bomb to ignite hydrogen fuel, creating an explosive force far greater than any earlier weapon. *(Library of Congress)*

"We have arrived at the point...where there is no real alternative to peace."

—President Dwight D. Eisenhower

because each nation involved would suffer devastation and a tremendous loss of life. Even if one nation launched a first attack, the other nation would still have enough nuclear weapons to strike back.

The scientist who had led the effort to develop the first atomic bomb during World War II, J. Robert Oppenheimer, said that the United States and the Soviet Union were like "two scorpions in a bottle, each capable of killing the other but only at the risk of his own life."

Because neither nation was going to get rid of its nuclear weapons, the U.S. military and government believed that the only way to keep the peace was to show the Soviets that the United States was prepared to fight a nuclear war—a strategy that came to be called deterrence. U.S. military leaders believed that nuclear weapons were also necessary because the Soviet Union had a much larger army than the United States and its allies in NATO had. Without the threat of a nuclear

DUCK AND COVER!

Despite the awesome destructive power of nuclear weapons, the federal Civil Defense Administration (CDA) worked to convince Americans that they could indeed survive a nuclear attack. The CDA produced a cartoon film featuring a character called Bert the Turtle, who taught schoolchildren to "duck and cover" if they saw the brilliant flash of a nuclear explosion. Air-raid drills, in which schoolchildren crawled under the desks or were sheltered in school basements, were a regular part of life for kids of the 1950s. Thousands of families dug up their backyards to build underground bomb shelters, built with steel and concrete, and stocked with food and water. Companies built heavy vaults to protect their records and drew up evacuation plans for their employees. The federal government considered creating a huge nationwide system of bomb shelters but decided it would be too expensive. Eventually the government and most Americans realized that there was little anyone could do to escape the horrors of a nuclear war if one were to start, and the shelter-building boom ended.

strike, many believed, the Soviets would use their superior forces to take over Western Europe.

Throughout the 1950s, the U.S. military developed technology to carry nuclear weapons to targets in the Soviet Union in the event of a war. The Strategic Air Command (SAC), part of the U.S. Air Force, built up a fleet of long-range jet bombers to carry nuclear weapons. At all times, some of these bombers were in the air, ready to strike.

The military also worked to find ways to protect the United States from nuclear attack during the 1950s. One important line of defense was the Distant Early Warning (DEW) line, a chain of radar stations that stretched 3,000 miles across the far north of Canada. The hope was that the DEW stations would detect attacking

A 1950s poster aimed at young schoolchildren depicts "one of six survival secrets for atomic attacks"—taking refuge in a bomb shelter. *(Library of Congress)*

Introduced in late 1953, the North American F-100 Super Sabre was the first U.S. military aircraft designed to fly faster than the speed of sound on a regular basis. Originally intended as a fighter, it was modified to carry bombs—including atomic bombs. *(Library of Congress)*

DDT

Many Americans of the 1950s were confident that science would create a better life for all people. Scientific advances, however, often create problems as well as solving them. Nuclear plants, for example, promise cheap energy, but they also produce radioactive waste that remains harmful for thousands of years. Another example is the use of the pesticide DDT. During World War II, DDT saved many lives overseas by killing the insects that carried diseases such as malaria and typhus. After the war, many farmers sprayed their fields with DDT. Few realized that the chemical also poisoned the birds that fed on insects, or that it could be harmful to humans. During the 1950s, naturalist Rachel Carson studied the effects of DDT on the environment. She later published her findings in *Silent Spring,* the 1962 book that marks the start of the environmental movement. *Silent Spring* led U.S. farmers to stop using DDT, though its use continues in some other countries.

Soviet bombers as they approached, in time to prevent them from bombing U.S. cities.

Some U.S. military leaders believed that missiles, rather than bombers, were the best way to carry nuclear weapons. Toward the end of World War II, Germany had developed a missile, the V-2 rocket, which was used against Britain. After the war, the U.S. Army brought many German rocket scientists and some captured V-2s to the United States. The military was interested in rockets for military purposes, but rockets also held the promise of helping humankind explore outer space.

It was known that the Soviets were also experimenting with rockets, but most Americans were confident that the U.S. program was much more advanced than the Soviet missile program. After all, the United States was considered the world leader in science and technology. The nation was home to most of the leading universities and research institutions in the world. The United States also had more top scientists—some of them refugees from Nazi Germany or from Communist countries—than any other country. The Soviet Union, on the other hand, was seen as inferior when it came to science and technology.

So it came as a huge surprise when, on October 5, 1957, a faint beeping sound was detected from radio waves coming from space. The sound came from *Sputnik*—the first satellite launched from Earth into space via a huge Soviet rocket. (*Sputnik* means "traveling companion" in Russian.)

The Soviet launching of *Sputnik* shocked Americans. Some called it a "technological Pearl Harbor." The supposedly inferior Soviet Union had beaten the United States in the race to enter outer space. If the Soviet Union had surpassed the United States in this area, Americans asked themselves, what else were the Soviets up to? Perhaps there was some truth to Khrushchev's boast that the Soviet Union would "bury" the United States.

In fact, *Sputnik* was not as remarkable an achievement as it first seemed. The satellite weighed only 184 pounds, and the batteries for its radio transmitter ran out after two weeks. The rocket that launched *Sputnik* was indeed crude compared to the models that the United States was working on.

Even so, *Sputnik* shook Americans' belief in American scientific superiority. Many Americans blamed the country's schools for lagging behind Soviet schools. Critics pointed out that Soviet students received more training in math and science than U.S. students. *Life* magazine claimed that the Soviet system "is producing many students better equipped with the technicalities of the Space Age."

Congress answered these criticisms by passing the National Defense Education Act in August 1958. The act provided $1 billion in funds for higher education, mostly in the form of scholarships for college and graduate students.

Sputnik also led the U.S. military to speed up its nuclear missile program. In response to the Soviet challenge, the United States rushed the Thor and Jupiter missiles into service in 1957. These weapons were ballistic missiles, which combined a rocket with a nuclear weapon, or warhead. In their testing phase, they were launched (without warheads) into space before plunging to their targets on Earth. These early missiles did not have the range to reach the Soviet Union from the United States, so they were stationed at bases in Europe.

Sputnik also marked the starting line of what would come to be called the space race between the United States and the Soviet Union. Two months after *Sputnik's* launch, the U.S. Navy attempted to get the first U.S. satellite into orbit atop a Vanguard rocket, but the rocket blew up seconds after liftoff at Cape Canaveral, Florida. On January 31, 1958, the first U.S. satellite, *Explorer 1,* was propelled into space aboard a Jupiter rocket.

Left to right: Scientists William Pickering, James Van Allen, and Wernher von Braun stand with a model of the rocket that lifted America's first satellite, *Explorer I,* into space in January 1958. *(Library of Congress)*

OTHER SCIENTIFIC DEVELOPMENTS

Despite losing the first contest of the space race, U.S. scientists and engineers were still in the lead in other areas in the 1950s. In the field of atomic energy, for example, the U.S. Navy launched the first nuclear-powered submarine, the USS *Nautilus,* in 1954. Four years later, the *Nautilus* became the first submarine to travel under the North Pole. Nuclear submarines could remain underwater for months without needing to surface to take on fuel, and they were almost impossible to detect. Armed with nuclear missiles that could be launched underwater, they made a powerful weapon in the ongoing campaign of deterrence against the Soviet Union. The first missile-carrying nuclear submarine, the USS *George Washington,* was commissioned in 1959. A year later, the navy launched a nuclear-powered aircraft carrier, the USS *Enterprise.*

After Congress passed the Atomic Energy Act of 1954, the U.S. Atomic Energy Commission pioneered the use of nuclear energy for the peaceful purpose of generating electrical power. Five years later, the first major

Workers at Remington Rand Corporation assemble one of the 46 UNIVAC I's produced between 1951 and 1958. At a cost of $1 million per computer, most were purchased by major corporations and used for accounting. *(Library of Congress)*

J. Presper Eckert (center) and reporter Walter Cronkite (right) with a UNIVAC I computer on election night, 1952. The UNIVAC made national headlines by correctly predicting (based on poll data) that Dwight Eisenhower would defeat Adlai Stevenson in the presidential race. *(Library of Congress)*

nuclear power plant went into service in Shippingport, Pennsylvania.

The United States also led the world in the new field of computer science. The first digital computers were built in the United States and Britain for military purposes during World War II, although the first powerful computer was the ENIAC (Electronic Numerical Integrator And Computer), completed in 1945 and ready for use in 1946.

The inventors of ENIAC, electrical engineer J. Presper Eckert and physicist John Mauchly, introduced an improved computer, the UNIVAC (Universal Automatic Computer) in 1951. Built by the Remington-Rand Corporation, the UNIVAC had a memory that could store programs and a keyboard to enter calculations. The UNIVAC could also print out its results on magnetic tape. The UNIVAC's first job was to help sort the data for the U.S. Census of 1950.

Early computers such as UNIVAC were very different than the personal computers that followed decades later. Because the first generation of computers used thousands of vacuum tubes to perform calculations, they were enormous machines. The UNIVAC was more than 14 feet in length and more than seven feet in height—

The computers of the 1950s were far less "user friendly" than today's personal computers: Monitors, mice, and graphical operating systems were years in the future.
(Library of Congress)

and they used huge amounts of power. Later in the 1950s, however, devices called transistors replaced the vacuum tubes, which made it possible to manufacture smaller computers that were even more powerful.

The introduction of the transistor led to the development of computers that businesses and universities could afford. Before the transistor, only the military and government agencies had the resources to pay for computers. In 1954, the International Business Machines Corporation (IBM) introduced the IBM 650, its first commercial business computer. The company sold more than 1,800 of these machines over the next few years, establishing IBM as the world's leading computer maker.

Early computers were very difficult to program. The development of new programming languages in the late 1950s, however, made it possible for people other than highly skilled mathematicians to operate computers. The first such language, Fortran, was introduced by IBM in 1954. Five years later, the first programming language designed for business use, COBOL (Common Business-Oriented Language) was released. The team that developed COBOL included Grace Murray Hopper, a lieutenant, and later a rear admiral in the U.S. Navy.

Another big leap in computer science came in 1958 with the introduction of the integrated circuit. Developed by two U.S. electrical engineers working independently of one another at the same time (Jack Kilby and Robert Noyce), the integrated circuit combined many electronic components on a single tiny wafer, or chip. Just as the transistor had replaced the vacuum tube, the integrated circuit soon replaced the transistor in computers and in many other electronic devices.

As in computer science, many of the advances in medical science during the 1950s had their roots in World War II. During the war, for example, frontline medics used penicillin on a large scale for the first time. Penicillin and similar drugs stopped infections in wounds that would otherwise have been fatal. These new drugs, known as antibiotics, also saved countless civilian lives after the war.

Open-heart surgery was another development with wartime roots. During World War II, Dr. Dwight Harken proved that surgeons could successfully operate on the heart. Such operations were very dangerous, however,without a way to slow the patient's heartbeat and blood circulation.

In the late 1940s and early 1950s, medical researchers developed a technique to slow heart action by cooling the body's temperature. In September 1952, two surgeons at the University of Minnesota used the new technique to operate on a five-year-old girl, who had been born with a hole in her heart. The successful operation marked the start of modern open-heart surgery. Another important development occurred in 1958 when scientists invented a machine that could do the work of the heart and lungs during surgery.

The biggest medical story of the 1950s was undoubtedly Dr. Jonas Salk's development of a vaccine for polio. Polio, or poliomyelitis, was one of the most dreaded diseases of the time. Caused by a virus, polio

"I have had dreams and I have had nightmares, but I have conquered my nightmares because of my dreams."

—Dr. Jonas Salk, developer of the first polio vaccine

At the height of the post–World War II polio epidemic, more than 60,000 Americans—most of them children—were stricken by the disease, and about 3,000 died. *(March of Dimes)*

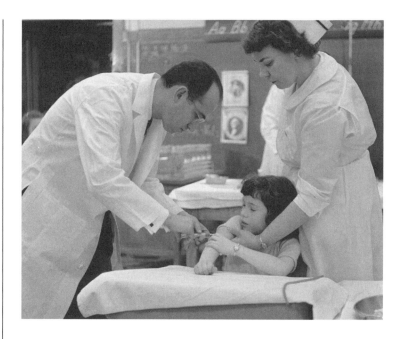

attacks the nerve cells of the spinal cord, which can lead to paralyzed limbs and death. The virus attacked children more than adults, although it spared no one—President Franklin Roosevelt lost the use of his legs to polio in 1921, at the age of 39.

Polio had puzzled scientists and terrified parents ever since it first appeared in the United States in 1916. While the rates of infection for most diseases fell during the twentieth century, the rate of polio infection rose. More than 33,000 Americans, most of them children, were infected in 1950. In 1952, polio killed more U.S. children than any other disease.

In the early 1950s, Dr. Salk was the director of the Virus Research Laboratory at the University of Pittsburgh Medical School. After experimenting to create vaccine for polio, he developed one that seemed very promising, but the vaccine needed to be tested on a large scale.

In 1954, people across the country took part in the effort to test the Salk vaccine. More than 20,000 doctors vaccinated over 600,000 schoolchildren. The doctors were helped by 64,000 teachers and more than 200,000 volunteers.

The massive test proved that the Salk vaccine worked and was safe. On April 12, 1955, the U.S. government approved the release of the vaccine. From then on, nearly every child in the United States was vaccinated against polio. The disease that people had feared for decades nearly disappeared within a few years, and Salk became a national hero.

ROCK IS DEAD, THEY SAY?

Rock 'n' roll had taken over the pop charts in the late 1950s, but by 1959, many of the leading rock 'n' rollers left the scene. In 1957, Little Richard decided to give up music to become a minister. Jerry Lee Lewis's popularity took a nosedive in 1958 when people learned that he had married his 13-year-old cousin. In that same year, Elvis was drafted into the U.S. Army for a two-year tour of duty. In 1959, Chuck Berry ran into trouble with the law and eventually went to jail. In February 1959, Buddy Holly died in a plane crash after a concert in Iowa. Mexican-American singer Richie Valens and DJ and singer J. P. "The Big Bopper" Richardson were also killed with Holly.

Rock 'n' roll did not disappear after 1959, but by the end of the decade it was dominated by performers such as Pat Boone, who recorded songs in a watered-down

WEST SIDE STORY

Many critics consider *West Side Story* (1957) to be the greatest musical of the decade. *West Side Story* teamed the brilliant classical composer and conductor Leonard Bernstein with Arthur Laurents (who wrote the original play), Stephen Sondheim (who wrote the lyrics to the songs), and Jerome Robbins (who directed the dance sequences). Although the musical was based on William Shakespeare's 16th-century tragedy *Romeo and Juliet*, *West Side Story* also reflected many aspects of city life in the 1950s. The story takes place in a section of New York City's Upper West Side neighborhood. (In the late 1950s, this area was being torn down to make room for the Lincoln Center complex of theaters and concert halls—an example of urban renewal.) The musical tells the story of the doomed love between a new arrival to New York, a Puerto Rican girl named Maria, and a local boy, Tony. The story of their relationship reflected the tensions between immigrants and the more established ethnic groups in cities like New York. *West Side Story* also mirrored public concern about juvenile delinquency in its portrayal of the fighting between gangs of teenage boys.

Joan Baez sang in coffehouses and other student hangouts in Palo Alto, California, and Boston, Massachusetts, before her performance at the 1959 Newport, Rhode Island, Folk Festival won her national attention. *(Library of Congress)*

Richard Knerr and Arthur "Spud" Melin founded the Wham-O Company in 1958 to market the Hula Hoop. That same year, Wham-O also introduced another wildly popular toy—the Frisbee. *(Library of Congress)*

style, and teen idols, such as Fabian, who were popular as much for their good looks as for their music. In the 1960s, however, musicians such as Bob Dylan, the Beatles, and the Rolling Stones would transform rock 'n' roll into rock music.

With the decline of rock 'n' roll, many young Americans turned to folk music. Played on acoustic instruments, folk was inspired by traditional U.S. music, from the ballads of the Appalachian Mountains to the blues of the Mississippi River Delta. The first big folk hit was the Kingston Trio's "Tom Dooley," which reached number one on the pop charts in 1958. Folk music was sometimes political: Pete Seeger, Joan Baez, and other performers wrote songs in support of the civil rights movement and the struggle for social justice.

FADS OF THE 1950S

The 1950s was a decade of fads that came and went quickly, a phenomenon that, because of TV, could spread from coast to coast in a matter of minutes. One of the biggest fads of the decade was the Hula Hoop, a large plastic ring that users swiveled around their bodies. The Hula Hoop had its origins in the bamboo hoops that Australian schoolchildren used in gym classes. The Wham-O Company in California heard about the hoops and introduced its version in 1958; by the end of the year Wham-O and other companies had sold more than 30 million. In the late 1950s, another popular fad swept college campuses as students competed to see how many people they could be cram into small spaces, such as phone booths and cars. Yet another fad was the use of chlorophyll, a chemical compound created by plants. Advertisers claimed that products with chlorophyll would give consumers sweet-smelling breath and stop other unpleasant odors. Soon chlorophyll was being added to many products, including toothpaste, deodorant, and dog food.

CHAPTER 6

THE END OF THE DECADE, 1958–1959

E ISENHOWER REMAINED A POPULAR president throughout his second term, but his administration was troubled. In September 1958, the president's chief of staff, Sherman Adams, resigned after he was accused of accepting gifts in return for political favors. In the same year, the unemployment rate rose for the first time in many years. This recession, or business downturn, did not last long, but it led people to worry about the nation's economy and their own financial security.

Supreme Court Chief Justice Earl Warren administers the Oath of Office to President Dwight Eisenhower on January 21, 1957. At the age of 66 as his second term began, Eisenhower was the oldest person elected to the presidency up to that time.
(Library of Congress)

A typical American family of the 1950s is shown with the food they will consume over the course of a year—much of it canned, frozen, and prepackaged. *(Library of Congress)*

"I want to talk about something besides kids and illnesses!"

—Bored suburbanite, in a cartoon by Dick Ericson

Some Americans already believed there was a dark underside to the nation's prosperity. There was public concern about the power of large companies and the relationship between corporations and the government. The 1950s was a time in which major corporations such as General Motors, IBM, and U.S. Steel dominated the economy. Some people believed that both Congress and the president paid more attention to the desires of business owners than to the needs of workers and poor Americans.

Many people also believed that the government was spending too much on defense, which caused the companies that made planes, missiles, and other military hardware to have too much influence on government policy. President Eisenhower himself warned against the rise of this "military-industrial complex" in a 1959 speech.

Other critics believed that Americans had become too materialistic—more interested in making money and buying goods than in improving their minds or helping others. Some people faulted advertisers for trying to convince Americans that buying a new car, television, or some other product would make them happier.

One influential critic of materialism was economist John Kenneth Galbraith. His book *The Affluent Society* (1958) argued that if the United States were to be a truly strong nation, the government needed to change its economic policies and spend more money on public services, such as health care and education.

The growing ranks of white-collar workers were also a concern for some thinkers. It seemed as if society expected that every young man's goal should be to get a job with a big company and work his way up the ladder to an executive position before retiring. (Women were expected to stay at home raising the children.)

The white-collar worker was expected to always agree with the boss, to spend his leisure time playing golf with his fellow employees or his company's customers, and generally be "a good company man." As writer William H. Whyte noted in his book *The Organization Man* (1956), creativity and individuality were usually not encouraged. No rising executive wanted to be accused of not being a team player.

This thinking led some white-collar workers to become lonely and depressed. Just as many women of the 1950s felt that there was something wrong with them for wanting a life beyond the home, many men wondered why a good salary, a nice house, and lots of possessions did not make them happy. This was the theme of Sloan Wilson's bestselling novel *The Man in the Gray Flannel Suit* (1955).

Canadian-born economist and social critic John Kenneth Galbraith, author of 1958's *The Affluent Society,* later served as U.S. ambassador to India. *(Library of Congress)*

"People very rarely think in groups; they talk together, they exchange information…they make compromises. But they do not think; they do not create."

—Sloan Wilson, author of *The Organization Man*, 1956

THE HIDDEN PERSUADERS

In 1957, social scientist Vance Packard published *The Hidden Persuaders,* a bestselling book about the role of advertising in U.S. society. In the book, Packard explores how television commercials and printed ads use consumers' fears about social acceptance and their body image to sell products. Packard also charges that some advertisers place hidden messages in their ads—images that are not easily noticeable, but that send signals to consumers' subconscious minds. This practice would come to be called "subliminal advertising," although Packard does not use the term in the book. In fact, later studies showed that such techniques were rare and usually did not work. Even so, *The Hidden Persuaders* helped alert consumers to the sophisticated psychology behind much modern advertising.

"The only people for me are the mad ones, the ones who are mad to live, mad to talk, mad to be saved..."

—From Jack Kerouac's *On the Road,* 1957

THE BEATS

One group who went against the grain of U.S. society in the 1950s was the Beats—a group of writers whose books began appearing in the mid-1950s. (To some Beat writers the term *Beat* referred to the group's belief that the average American was "beaten down" by U.S. society. To others, including writer Jack Kerouac, the group's name was connected to their view that nature is "beatific," or blessed.)

Instead of conformity, the *Beats* championed individuality. They rejected materialism and the white-collar life in favor of a more spiritual, creative existence. The Beats were attracted to people outside the mainstream of society, such as African-American jazz musicians, whose slang they borrowed. Some of the Beats looked to Asian religions, especially Zen Buddhism, for inspiration.

The Beats began to attract attention in 1955, when the young poet Allen Ginsberg read aloud his long poem "Howl" at the Six Gallery in San Francisco. Two years later, Jack Kerouac turned the Beats into a full-fledged phenomenon when he published his novel *On the Road,* a fictionalized account of his travels across the United States. Other notable Beat writers included the poets Lawrence Ferlinghetti and Gregory Corso and the novelists John Clellon Holmes and William S. Burroughs.

Eager to take up the Beats' message of individual freedom and creative expression, thousands of young people flocked to Beat hangouts, such as New York City's Greenwich Village and San Francisco's North Beach. (Inspired by *Sputnik,* San Francisco journalist Herb Caen coined the term *Beatnik* to describe these young people.) Many of their parents were not as enthusiastic about the movement. Some Beat writing, especially Ginsberg's "Howl," was considered obscene. (Ginsberg was gay, and during the 1950s most Americans disapproved of homosexuality.) The

JACK KEROUAC

The author of the so-called Beat Bible, *On the Road,* Jack Kerouac was born Jean-Louis Kerouac in Lowell, Massachusetts, in 1922. The son of descendants of French-Canadian immigrants, Kerouac grew up speaking French at home. He attended New York's Columbia University, where he met Allen Ginsberg, William S. Burroughs, and other figures who became leaders of the Beat movement. In 1950, Kerouac published his first novel, *The Town and the City,* but it did not attract much attention. He traveled widely and worked at a variety of jobs until winning fame for *On the Road* in 1957. Kerouac said he wrote the novel in just three weeks, typing on a single roll of paper. (Another novelist, Truman Capote, commented, "That's not writing—that's just typing.") Kerouac continued to publish fiction, including *The Dharma Bums* (1958) and *Doctor Sax* (1959). He also published a volume of poetry, *Mexico City Blues* (1959), but his later books did not match the success of *On the Road.* Kerouac became uncomfortable with his role as King of the Beats, and loneliness and heavy drinking marked his later years. He died in 1967 at the age of 47.

Beats' use of marijuana and other drugs also disturbed many people.

By the end of the decade, a watered-down version of the Beat lifestyle became a fad. In the popular mind, the Beatnik was a young person who wore a black turtleneck sweater and a beret, and who hung around in dingy cafés playing the bongo drums. The popular television show *The Many Loves of Dobie Gillis* even introduced a Beatnik character named Maynard G. Krebs.

Although the original Beat writers continued to publish, the movement soon faded out. Yet the Beats left a deep mark on U.S. culture. Their approach to life and the ideas they expressed in their writings would be a major influence on the young Americans of the 1960s.

EISENHOWER CONTINUES TO CONTAIN COMMUNISM

In July 1958, a revolution in Iraq threatened to spill over into the neighboring nations of Jordan, Syria, and Lebanon. Eisenhower responded by ordering 5,000 U.S. troops to Lebanon. Although the Soviet Union and several Arab nations protested, the crisis passed and the U.S. troops went home.

"I saw the best minds of my generation destroyed by madness, starving hysterical naked..." So began Allen Ginsberg's 1955 poem "Howl," which helped turn the Beats from a small literary movement into a national phenomenon. Ginsberg is shown here later in life. *(Library of Congress)*

Chiang Kai-shek (1887–1975) was the Nationalist Chinese leader who ruled Taiwan during the crisis over Quemoy and Matsu. *(Library of Congress)*

On the other side of the world, the United States also acted forcefully to keep the peace. After the Communist victory in mainland China in 1949, the anticommunist Chinese leader Chiang Kai-shek, whom the United States supported, moved his government to the offshore island of Formosa (Taiwan).

In 1958, guns from the People's Republic of China (Communist China) began firing on Quemoy and Matsu, two small Formosan-controlled islands off the Chinese coast. Eisenhower ordered the U.S. Navy's Seventh Fleet to take up a position between Formosa and the mainland. The purpose of the action was to stop the Chinese from shelling Quemoy and Matsu, and also to discourage Chiang from carrying out threats to launch military raids on the mainland. As was true of the Suez Crisis, the Quemoy-Matsu situation showed that despite U.S. opposition to communism, the Eisenhower administration was not willing to let small crises flare up into major wars.

In Southeast Asia, however, the situation was more complicated. Under the terms of the 1955 agreement that ended France's war in Indochina, North and South Vietnam were supposed to reunite following free elections. In 1956, however, South Vietnam refused to hold the planned elections. The United States supported South Vietnam's decision.

Soon afterward, communist guerrillas began fighting against the South Vietnamese government, with help from communist-ruled North Vietnam. Fighting also flared up in the neighboring nation of Laos. The United States increased shipments of military aid to South Vietnam and sent U.S. forces to advise and train the South Vietnamese and Laotian armies.

In 1959, two U.S. advisers died in a roadside ambush in South Vietnam. No one could foresee it at the time, but they were the first U.S. deaths in what would become the longest war in the nation's history, a conflict that would deeply divide Americans. More than 58,000

Americans died in Southeast Asia before the United States finally withdrew from Vietnam in 1973.

The United States also had to deal with troubles closer to home during Eisenhower's second term. Anti-U.S. feeling ran high in Latin America in the 1950s. Many people in the region remained angry at the CIA's actions in Guatemala in 1953. They also resented the fact that the U.S. government was on friendly terms with cruel, anticommunist rulers such as Raphael Trujillo in the Dominican Republic and Anastasio Somoza in Nicaragua. Latin Americans also opposed the overbearing influence of U.S. corporations, such as the United Fruit Company, on local economies.

The depth of Latin American anger at the United States was not really understood at home until Vice President Richard Nixon toured several Latin American countries in 1958. In some places Nixon received a warm welcome. In others, angry crowds spat and threw rocks at him. In Caracas, the capital of Venezuela, Nixon and his wife barely escaped harm when a mob attacked their car.

The Eisenhower administration tried to improve U.S.-Latin American relations later that year by setting up the Inter-American Development Bank, which provided loans to Latin American nations to help develop their economies. Congress also increased the amount of aid to Latin America in an effort to help fight widespread there.

In January 1959, rebels led by the young revolutionary leader Fidel Castro overthrew Fulgencio Batista's dictatorship in Cuba. Castro's promise to bring democracy to Cuba won him much goodwill in the United States.

Not long after taking power, however, Castro imprisoned and killed people whom he considered his enemies. He also seized U.S. property in Cuba. Even more worrying to U.S. leaders, Castro spoke approvingly of Soviet-style communism and sought aid from the Soviet Union.

As the decade ended, Castro was well on his way to turning Cuba into a pro-Soviet dictatorship, and

Soviet premiere Nikita Khrushchev meets Cuban dictator Fidel Castro for the first time at the United Nations in 1960. By this time the Soviet Union and Cuba were firm allies, much to the dismay of the U.S. government. *(Library of Congress)*

hundreds of thousands of Cubans fled to the United States. Castro's move into the Soviet camp was especially troubling because Cuba was so close to the United States—less than 100 miles separated the island nation from the coast of Florida. Cuba remained a thorn in the side of the United States even after the cold war ended, when Castro continued to rule one of the world's last remaining communist nations.

CONFLICTS WITH THE SOVIET UNION CONTINUE

While the United States dealt with crises around the world, the Eisenhower administration continued to confront the Soviet Union in Europe. U.S. and West European leaders had hoped that Nikita Khrushchev's rise to power in the Soviet Union would lead to a permanent thaw in the cold war. They were especially encouraged when word leaked out that Khrushchev had criticized the brutal rule of his predecessor, Joseph Stalin, in a secret speech to Communist Party members.

In 1956, a spirit of revolt spread in several nations behind the Iron Curtain. When local leaders in Poland demanded greater self-government, Khrushchev surprised Western leaders by agreeing to some of their demands.

Encouraged, the people of Hungary demanded not only local rule but complete independence from Soviet control. Khrushchev responded by sending the Soviet army into Hungary. The result was a bloodbath as Soviet tanks rolled through the streets of Hungary's capital, Budapest. Soviet soldiers hunted down and killed the brave but poorly armed rebels, thus stopping the revolt.

The next crisis came over Berlin. Although located inside communist-ruled East Germany, the city was still divided into zones controlled by the United States, France, and Britain (West Berlin) and the Soviet Union (East Berlin). Because of this situation, East Germans who wanted to flee communist rule traveled to West Berlin and then moved on to new lives in democratic, prosperous West Germany. Some 3 million East Germans migrated to West Germany between 1949 and 1958.

In November 1958, Khrushchev was alarmed by the drain of East German citizens to the West. He demanded that the United States, Britain, and France withdraw from Berlin or risk war. President Eisenhower decided that the situation was so serious that it could only be resolved by a personal meeting with the Soviet leader. In September 1959, Khrushchev became the first Soviet leader to visit the United States.

Khrushchev went on a 10-day tour of the country, including visits to an Iowa farm and California. He became angry when he learned that he could not visit Disneyland for security reasons. "Have gangsters taken over the place?" he asked.

After his cross-country tour, Khrushchev met with Eisenhower at Camp David, the official presidential retreat in Maryland's Catoctin Mountains. While the two leaders did not come to an immediate agreement over

Tough, earthy Nikita Khrushchev (1894–1971) ruled the Soviet Union from 1953 until 1964. *(Library of Congress)*

Berlin, they promised to solve the problem peacefully, and they agreed to meet again in Paris in May 1960.

After the meeting, Americans began to speak of "the spirit of Camp David" in U.S.-Soviet relations. Many hoped that the upcoming summit meeting in Paris would not only lead to a settlement over Berlin, but would also begin an era of peaceful cooperation between the United States and the Soviet Union.

These hopes were shattered on May 1, 1960, when a Soviet anti-aircraft missile shot down a U.S. U-2 spy plane flying high over Soviet territory. The U-2's pilot, a CIA employee named Francis Gary Powers, bailed out and was captured by the Soviets.

At first, the Eisenhower administration claimed that the U-2 had simply gone off course after taking off from Pakistan on a flight to take weather readings. The Soviets, however, were able to prove that the U-2's cameras had photographed Soviet military bases.

Khrushchev and Eisenhower went ahead with their meeting in Paris, but the spirit of Camp David was gone. Eisenhower promised to stop the U-2 flights over the Soviet Union, but that pledge did not satisfy a furious Khrushchev. He left the meeting early to return to Moscow, although he did express the hope that the so-called U-2 Incident would be, in his words, a "passing phase" in U.S.-Soviet relations. The two superpowers had managed to avoid war once again, but the U-2 Incident began a chilly period of the cold war that lasted for more than a decade.

MOVIES, THEATER, AND THE VISUAL ARTS

For Hollywood, the 1950s was a tough decade. Competition from television led to falling ticket sales. Many of the major movie studios suffered serious financial trouble during these years.

To bring more people out of their living rooms and back into the theaters, Hollywood made moviegoing a

3-D MOVIES AND SMELL-O-VISION

One of the gimmicks that moviemakers turned to in the 1950s was a 3-D, or three-dimensional, movie. Developed by the Natural Image Corporation, 3-D movies projected a number of images at the same time. When audiences viewed the movies through special glasses, the technology gave an illusion of depth to the action onscreen. In fact, the 3-D process made it seem as if objects in the movie were moving from the screen toward the audience. The first major 3-D film, *Bwana Devil,* a horror movie about a killer lion, opened in late 1952 and was an immediate hit. The new technique's popularity was short-lived, however, because most 3-D movies were not very well made or interesting. An even less successful gimmick was Smell-O-Vision, which pumped different scents into the movie audience's seating area.

Marlon Brando played Johnny Stabler, leader of the Black Rebels motorcycle gang in 1953's *The Wild One.* The movie was inspired by a real-life episode that took place in Hollister, California, years earlier. *(Library of Congress)*

richer experience by adding big screens and stereo sound, which televisions of the 1950s did not offer. The studios also adopted new film technologies to improve the movie picture. Cinerama was a technology that used three projectors and a huge screen to create a highly detailed image. Most Cinerama movies, however, were short films or travelogues about exotic places around the world. Hollywood made only two full-length movies for the system. Another wide-screen system, CinemaScope, which included four-channel stereo sound, was more successful. By the end of the 1950s, most major movies used the Panavision wide-screen system, or similar methods. The number of movies made in color rather than black-and-white also rose in the 1950s.

The studios also began producing lavish, star-studded movies that television could not match. Many

"Movies are better than ever!"

—Slogan from a Hollywood advertising campaign

The Creature from the Black Lagoon stalks away with his beautiful victim in this scene from the 1954 movie of the same name. Low-budget science fiction and horror films were a staple of drive-in movie theaters. *(Library of Congress)*

of these big-budget epics had religious or historical themes, such as *The Robe* (1953), *The Ten Commandments* (1956), and *Ben-Hur* (1959).

At the other end of the scale, the 1950s also saw the release of many cheaply made movies aimed at a teenage audience, from horror movies such as *The Creature from the Black Lagoon* (1954) and *I Was a Teenage Werewolf* (1957), to rock 'n' roll-themed movies such as *High School Confidential* (1957) and *Don't Knock the Rock* (1958). The nation's top rock 'n' roll star, Elvis Presley, went to Hollywood to star in a 1956 drama, *Love Me Tender.* He made 30 more movies over the next 13 years.

In the mid-1950s, Hollywood and the television industry began to cooperate instead of competing. In the early 1950s, the movie studios had banned their stars from appearing in television productions. When the ban was lifted in 1956, popular movie and television performers moved freely between the big screen and the small screen. Some movies even started out as television shows, most notably the 1953 television drama *Marty*. The movie version of *Marty* won the Academy Award for Best Picture in 1956.

After the new technology of videotape was introduced, movie studios were able to produce shows for the television networks. The studios also sold the networks the rights to broadcast movies that had been released before 1948.

Two of the biggest stars to come out of Hollywood in the1950s were Marlon Brando and Marilyn Monroe. In 1947, Brando's performance as Stanley Kowalski in Tennessee Williams's play *A Streetcar Named Desire* created a sensation on Broadway. In 1951, he brought the role to the big screen, to wide acclaim. Brando was part of a new generation of actors trained in the Stanislavski Method, a system of acting that emphasized emotion.

Oklahoma!, the Broadway smash musical of 1943, came to the big screen in 1955. "Now everyone can see it—at popular prices!" proclaimed posters advertising the movie. *(Library of Congress)*

A real cliffhanger: Jimmy Stewart starred in several of director Alfred Hitchcock's thrillers, including 1958's *Vertigo,* in which he played a detective with a fear of heights. *(Library of Congress)*

His acting in two later movies, *The Wild One* (1953) and *On the Waterfront* (1954), had a power that had rarely been seen before in the movies.

In *The Wild One,* Brando seemed to challenge the conformity of the 1950s in his performance as Johnny, the leader of a gang of motorcycle-riding outlaws who take over a small California town. In one famous scene, a waitress asks Johnny what he's rebelling against. "Whaddaya got?" he sneers in reply. Brando's later career included some bad as well as some great movies, and he had a troubled personal life, but by his death in 2004, he was considered by many critics to be the most influential actor of his generation.

Marilyn Monroe, born Norma Jean Mortenson in 1926, acted in small parts before rising to stardom in *Gentlemen Prefer Blondes* (1953). The title of that movie sums up the plots of the comedies she starred in. In *The Seven-Year Itch* (1955) and *Some Like It Hot* (1959), she plays a woman who dazzles men with her beauty but remains innocent at heart. Monroe broke out of this mold with a powerful dramatic performance in the movie version of William Inge's play *Bus Stop* (1956).

Like Marlon Brando, Marilyn Monroe's personal life was often troubled, and her off-screen personality was very different from the sweet, sunny characters she played in most of her movies. In 1954, she married a leading baseball player, Joe DiMaggio, which led to divorce within a year. She later married the great playwright, Arthur Miller, but that marriage was also short-lived. She died of a drug overdose in 1962 at the age of 36.

Perhaps the greatest movie director of the 1950s was Alfred Hitchcock. The British-born Hitchcock directed a series of thrillers that were smart, sophisticated, and filled with suspense and surprising plot twists, including *Rear Window* (1954), *Vertigo* (1958), and *North By Northwest* (1959). *Rear Window* starred Grace Kelly, who made headlines when she left the movies to

THE GUGGENHEIM MUSEUM

In architecture, urban office and apartment buildings of the 1950s were usually built in the International Style, which developed before World War II. Buildings constructed in this style were tall, steel-framed structures with glass walls. They were simple in form with little or no decoration. Chicago's Lake Shore Drive Apartments, completed in 1951 and designed by the German-born architect Ludwig Mies van der Rohe is one famous example of the International Style. Another is New York City's Seagram Building, completed in 1958 by van der Rohe and U.S. architect Philip Johnson. One of the greatest buildings of the 1950s, however, was the work of an architect who had started his career in the 1890s: Frank Lloyd Wright. The building was the Guggenheim Museum in New York City. In his plans for the Guggenheim, Wright broke all the rules of traditional museum design. Instead of displaying art in a series of small galleries, the spiral-shaped Guggenheim places the artworks on the curved walls of the building itself. Visitors start at the top level of the museum and view the artworks by walking down a continuous curved ramp. Construction began in 1956 and the museum opened in 1959, three months after Wright's death at the age of 91.

Not all architecture critics liked Frank Lloyd Wright's nontraditional design for the Guggenheim Museum: One wrote that the building "[is] a war between architecture and painting in which both come out badly maimed." *(Library of Congress)*

Director Francois Truffaut was a leader of the innovative new wave (*nouvelle vague,* in French) movement in French filmmaking in the 1950s and 1960s. Other new wave directors whose films were well received in America included Louis Malle and Jean-Luc Godard. *(Library of Congress)*

become a real-life princess. In 1956 she married Prince Rainier of the tiny European principality of Monaco.

In 1960, Hitchcock surprised audiences by directing a different kind of movie, the thriller *Psycho.* The famous shower scene, in which the character played by Janet Leigh is brutally murdered by the character played by Anthony Perkins, was so terrifying to some moviegoers that they were said to be afraid to take showers for days after seeing the movie.

One unexpected result of the competition between television and Hollywood in the 1950s was a new interest in movies made overseas. As U.S. studios made fewer movies, theater owners turned to foreign films to fill their seats. The 1950s was a time of great creativity in filmmaking around the world, and U.S. audiences enjoyed masterpieces by directors such as Japan's Akira Kurosawa (*Rashomon,* 1951), Sweden's Ingmar Bergman (*The Seventh Seal,* 1956), France's Francois Truffaut (*The 400 Blows,* 1958) and India's Satyajit Ray (*The World of Apu,* 1959).

Among the most successful movie imports of the decade was the French film *And God Created Woman* (1957), directed by Roger Vadim and starring the beautiful Brigitte Bardot. Many Americans considered the movie indecent, and some communities banned it, but that did not stop the film from earning $4 million in the United States, a huge sum at the time.

THE THEATER, BALLET, AND THE VISUAL ARTS

Musicals were the big attraction on Broadway in the 1950s. Plays that combined song and dance with drama and comedy had been around since the 1920s, but in

1943, *Oklahoma!* raised the musical to the level of a U.S. art form. *Oklahoma!* was the work of Richard Rodgers (who wrote the music) and Oscar Hammerstein II (who wrote the lyrics). The team of Rodgers and Hammerstein continued to produce hit musicals in the 1950s, from *The King and I* (1951) to *The Sound of Music* (1959).

Rodgers and Hammerstein had competition from another team, Frederick Loewe and Alan Jay Lerner. Their musical *My Fair Lady,* inspired by British writer George Bernard Shaw's play *Pygmalion,* was the most popular musical of the decade. It opened in 1956 and ran for nine years. Another popular musical of the 1950s was Meredith Wilson's *The Music Man* (1957).

In drama, the playwrights Arthur Miller and Tennessee Williams dominated the 1950s, as they had the 1940s. In 1953, Miller created controversy with his play, *The Crucible.* The play was based on an actual event, the Salem Witch Trials of 1692, when innocent people in colonial Massachusetts were put to death after being accused of witchcraft. Many people understood that the play was meant to be viewed as commentary on the activities of Senator Joseph McCarthy and his hunt for supposed communists. Williams also explored controversial themes in his plays, *The Glass Menagerie* (1950) and *Cat on a Hot Tin Roof* (1955).

The 1950s also saw the rise in what came to be called off-Broadway theater, as small playhouses, in New York City neighborhoods such as Greenwich Village, put on less expensive productions. The big off-Broadway hit of the decade was a musical, *The Threepenny Opera,* by German playwright Bertolt Brecht and songwriter Kurt Weill, which opened in 1955. One of the songs from the show, "Mack the Knife," became a surprise hit on the pop charts for singer Bobby Darin.

In ballet, choreographer, or dance designer, Martha Graham's fierce, emotional approach broke with the more formal styles of the past. Graham's company, the Martha Graham School for Contemporary Dance, had

The first African-American choreographer to win nationwide fame, Alvin Ailey studied with Martha Graham and danced in Broadway and off-Broadway productions before founding his own dance troupe in 1959. *(Library of Congress)*

a huge influence on ballet not only in America, but also around the world. In 1955, when she was 61 years old, Graham amazed audiences with her performance in *The Seraphic Dialogues,* which is now considered one of her greatest works of choreography.

One of Graham's students, Alvin Ailey, would also have a big impact on the world of dance. He scored a major success in 1958 with *Blues Suite,* after which he founded the Alvin Ailey Dance Company, the first U.S. African-American dance troupe.

In the world of the visual arts, the most famous U.S. art movement of the decade was abstract impressionism, a style that began in New York City in the 1940s. Sometimes called action painters, the abstract impressionists created bold works filled with swirls or blocks of color. The leading abstract impressionist, Jackson Pollock, was nicknamed "Jack the Dripper" for the way he dripped and hurled paint across his huge canvases. Other notable abstract impressionists included Mark Rothko, Robert Motherwell, and Willem de Kooning.

The late 1950s also saw the rise of pop art, a style that used ordinary objects as the starting point for artistic expression. In the 1950s, the leading artist in the style was Jasper Johns, who first gained fame in 1957 for a series of paintings of U.S. flags.

"It's just like a bed of flowers. You don't have to tear your hair out over what it means."

—Jackson Pollock
on his paintings

CHAPTER 7

THE EDGE OF THE NEW FRONTIER, 1960

IN THE 1950s AND INTO THE 1960s, MANY Americans who lived in rural areas were left behind by the long boom. In a way, the nation's farmers were victims of their own success. Improved fertilizers and farm machinery, such as mechanical harvesters, doubled the amount of corn, cotton, and wheat produced between 1950 and 1960.

With crops flooding the market, their prices fell, which made it hard for farmers to pay back the money they had borrowed from banks to pay for the new

Black and white students attend an integrated public-school classroom in Washington, D.C. America's schools were increasingly integrated as the 1950s ended, but many states still resisted the Supreme Court's order to integrate their school systems "with all deliberate speed." *(Library of Congress)*

machines and fertilizers. Between 1953 and 1960, about 5 million farm families could not afford to stay on their land and were forced to find other work. They were replaced by big companies, which hired laborers at low wages to farm hundreds of thousands of acres of land. These large company farms could afford the fertilizers and machinery needed to make a profit.

To help the nation's remaining small farmers, the federal government introduced a system of price supports. This program paid farmers not to produce certain crops. In 1956, the government started the Soil Bank plan, which paid farmers not to plant any crops at all on some of their land. Despite these programs, the number of family farms continued to fall.

For U.S. labor unions, the 1950s were both the best of times and the worst of times. In 1953, union membership reached an all-time high: In that year, about one-third of all U.S. workers belonged to unions. Two years later, two of the nation's leading union organizations, the Congress of Industrial Organizations (CIO) and the American Federation of Labor (AFL), joined together to form the AFL-CIO. The new group had a membership of more than 16 million workers.

On the negative side, government committees found that some unions were linked to organized crime or were otherwise corrupt. In 1957, for example, the AFL-CIO threw out the Teamsters Union for the misuse of pension funds and ties to organized crime. In 1959, Congress passed the Labor-Management Reporting and Disclosure Act, better known as the Landrum-Griffin Act, which aimed to reduce union corruption by regulating the election of union officials, among other measures.

Throughout the 1950s, improved technology meant that fewer workers were needed to produce industrial goods. More and more, the nation's factories used machines to do the work of people—a process called automation. The growing use of computers also cut down on the number of workers needed in factories and shops.

Automation was one of the reasons 500,000 steel-workers went out on strike on July 15, 1959, beginning the longest strike in the history of the steel industry. For 116 days the strike halted 90 percent of U.S. steel production. Finally, on November 7, the U.S. Supreme Court ordered the strikers back to work for 80 days while union officials and company management negotiated a settlement with help from the federal government. (The Court halted the strike under the terms of the 1947 Taft-Hartley Act, which allowed the court to stop strikes that endangered "national health or safety.") The steel companies and the union reached a settlement in January, but the strike had gone on for so long that some U.S. manufacturers had started to use steel imported from overseas.

In other industries, strong sales of products meant that some companies could afford to keep employees on the payroll even as automation took over many jobs. In 1955, for example, the United Auto Workers union, (UAW), negotiated a contract with auto manufacturers that guaranteed an annual wage. This guarantee meant that even if car sales fell and the auto manufacturers had to lay off workers, the laid-off workers would still get paid.

In a prosperous economy, however, many workers decided that they did not need union membership to protect their jobs and benefits. By the end of the 1950s, union membership began a decline that continued into the 21st century.

SPORTS IN THE 1950S

Baseball remained the most popular spectator sport in the 1950s. After Jackie Robinson broke the major leagues' color bar in 1947, more and more talented African-American players signed with the American

Catcher Roy Campanella followed Jackie Robinson onto the Brooklyn Dodgers's roster to become one of Major League Baseball's first African-American players. He earned three Most Valuable Player awards before injuries from a 1958 car accident cut his career short. *(Library of Congress)*

The New York Yankees's legendary Number Seven, Mickey Mantle used his bat to help the team to pennant victories from 1951 through 1953 and again from 1955 through 1958, plus World Series victories in 1956 and 1958. *(Library of Congress)*

Outfielder Larry Doby of the Cleveland Indians became the first African-American player in the American League. *(Library of Congress)*

and National league teams. They included future Hall-of-Famers Larry Doby (center fielder for the Cleveland Indians, 1947–59), Roy Campanella (catcher for the Brooklyn Dodgers from 1948 until a car accident left him paralyzed in 1958), and the dazzling Willie Mays, the "Say Hey Kid," who began his major league career with the New York Giants in 1951 and retired from the New York Mets in 1973 with 2,383 hits and 660 home runs. The all-time home-run hitter (as of 2005), Hank Aaron, also got his major league start in the 1950s, joining the Milwaukee Braves in 1954.

The integration of major league baseball also led to the end of the Negro Leagues, which had flourished from the 1880s into the 1950s. Some great Negro League stars made the transition to the major leagues, including Leroy "Satchel" Paige, who was called up by the Cleveland Indians in 1948 and later played for the St. Louis Browns and the Kansas City Athletics. No one, Satchel included, knew his exact birth date, but he was in his forties when drafted by the Indians, which made him the oldest rookie ever to hit the majors. He was close to 60 when he retired in 1965.

The American League's New York Yankees dominated the decade on the diamond, thanks to the leadership of manager Casey Stengel and a lineup that included catcher Yogi Berra, outfielder Mickey Mantle, and pitcher Whitey Ford. The Yankees seemed practically unbeatable during the 1950s, winning the league pennant nine times and the World Series six times between 1950 and 1960.

In addition to integration, major league baseball in the 1950s reflected another trend in U.S. society—the westward movement of Americans from the East Coast. In 1950, St. Louis, Missouri, was the only city west of the Mississippi River that had a major-league team. In 1953, the Boston Braves moved to Milwaukee, Wisconsin. (They would later move to Atlanta, Georgia.) Two years later, the Philadelphia Athletics moved to

DON LARSEN'S PERFECT GAME

Perhaps the most unforgettable moment in sports of the 1950s sports came on October 8, 1956. It was the fifth game of the World Series, with the New York Yankees facing the Brooklyn Dodgers at Brooklyn's Ebbets Field. The series was tied, with each team having won two games, when pitcher Don Larsen took the mound for the Yankees. Ninty-seven pitches later, Larsen stepped down after retiring 27 hitters. It was the first perfect game in the major leagues since 1922 and the only perfect game in a World Series as of 2004. (The Yankees went on to take the series in seven games.) In the words of sportswriter Shirley Povich, "The million-to-one shot came in. "What makes Larsen's feat even more remarkable is the fact that his career, both before and after that game, was not particularly distinguished. When he retired in 1967, his record, with six teams, was only 81–91 (wins–losses). For one amazing day, however, Larsen was just perfect.

Nicknamed the Golden Arm, Johnny Unitas of the Baltimore Colts was the greatest quarterback of the 1950s, and perhaps of all time, in the opinion of many football fans and sportswriters. *(Library of Congress)*

Kansas City, Missouri. (They would move farther west to Oakland, California in 1968.)

In 1958, California got its first major league teams when the New York Giants relocated to San Francisco, and when the scrappy Brooklyn Dodgers broke their devoted fans' hearts by abandoning legendary Ebbets Field for Los Angeles.

Integration was achieved in other sports, too. In 1950, Althea Gibson became the first African-American tennis player to enter the U.S. Open in Forest Hills, New York. Six years later she won the French Open, and in 1957 and 1958 Gibson won both the women's singles and doubles championships at Wimbledon in England, and the U.S. Open singles at Forest Hills.

Baseball may have been the most popular sport in the 1950s, but it now had serious competition from professional football and basketball. Football's popularity rose in 1950, when the game first allowed unlimited substitution of players. This change led to more exciting play and a greater role for coaches. At the time, there were two major professional football organizations, the National Football League (NFL) and the All-American

"Age is a question of mind over matter. If you don't mind, it doesn't matter."

—Satchel Paige, the oldest rookie in major league baseball

WILMA RUDOLPH

In the 1950s, Wilma Glodean Rudolph broke through barriers of race, class, and sex to become one of the outstanding track-and-field athletes of all time. She was born into a poor African-American family in Tennessee in 1940. (She was one of 22 children.) Rudolph suffered many illnesses as a child, including polio, and she could not walk without a leg brace or crutches until she was 12. Despite these difficulties, she became a star basketball player and sprinter in high school. In 1956, at the age of 16, she won a bronze medal in the 100-meter relay at the Olympic Games in Melbourne, Australia. Her greatest achievements came four years later at the Rome Olympics, when she became the first woman from the United States to win three gold medals for track-and-field events while also tying the world record in the 100-meter dash. After retiring from competition in the 1960s, Rudolph worked to promote women's track-and-field. She was elected to the United States Olympic Hall of Fame in 1983.

Wilma Rudolph (center) celebrates during medal ceremonies at the 1960 Olympics in Rome. *(Library of Congress)*

Football Association (AAFC), although as the decade went on most of the AAFC teams moved to the NFL.

The 1958 NFL league championship game pitted the New York Giants against the Baltimore Colts. It was the first football game to be broadcast on national television, the first to be decided in overtime, and, in the opinion of many sports historians, it marked the start of the modern era in professional football. This game remains one of the most exciting NFL games of all time.

Modern professional basketball began in 1949, when the Basketball Association of America (BAA) and the National Basketball League (NBL) merged to form the NBA (National Basketball Association). The dominant NBA team of the early 1950s was the Minneapolis Lakers from Minnesota. Center George Mikan led the Lakers to five NBA championships between 1949 and 1955. (In 1960, the Lakers moved to Los Angeles.)

In the mid-1950s, guard Bob Cousy put the Boston Celtics in the forefront of the NBA, helping to win championships in 1957 and every year from 1959 to 1963. The 1950s Celtics also included the great Bill Russell, who joined the team in 1956 after winning a gold medal for the United States in the Olympic Games.

Another outstanding player of the 1950s was forward Bob Pettit of the St. Louis Hawks, who helped his team win the NBA championship in 1958. Wilt Chamberlain, one of the all-time greats, entered professional basketball in 1958 with the Harlem Globetrotters exhibition team before moving to the Philadelphia Warriors in 1959.

Boxing was another popular sport in the 1950s. Unlike previous decades, middleweight boxing provided more excitement than heavyweight matches. The best boxer of the era was probably Walker Smith Jr., better known as Sugar Ray Robinson. After winning 91 straight fights as a welterweight, Robinson moved to the middleweight class in 1951 and successfully defended his title as world champion five times between 1951 and 1960.

Standing 6' 10", Bill Russell's brilliance at defensive play for the Boston Celtics gave the team 11 NBA championships between 1957 and 1969.
(Library of Congress)

THE QUIZ SHOW SCANDAL

Television quiz shows, in which contestants win money for correctly answering questions on a variety of subjects, were all the rage in the 1950s. One of the most popular shows was NBC's *Twenty One,* which was based on the card game blackjack. In November 1956, a handsome young university professor, Charles Van Doren, made his first appearance as a contestant on the show. Over the next few days, Van Doren won $129,000 while in competition with college student Herbert Stempel. The show made Van Doren a national celebrity. Approximately 50 million people watched his final appearance on the show, and he made the cover of *Time* magazine. Later, in 1958, Herbert Stempel claimed that *Twenty One* was rigged: Stempel charged that the show's producers had decided in advance who would win and who would lose. He also said that they coached contestants to act in a way that made it seem as if the on-screen action was a real competition. Contestants from other popular quiz shows came forward to report similar stories. The accusations caused a national outcry. Both a New York jury and a Congressional committee investigated the charges and found them to be true. As for Van Doren, he first claimed to be innocent, but finally admitted that he was involved in the deception. The scandal led to the cancellation of many shows and a federal law against rigging quiz shows.

Charles Van Doren during one of his 14 appearances on *Twenty One.* After his confession, two big winners on another popular quiz show, *The $64,000 Question,* came forward to admit that they too had taken part in cheating on the program. *(Library of Congress)*

In the heavyweight class, the 1950s belonged to Rocco "Rocky" Marciano, who beat "Jersey Joe" Walcott (born Arnold Cream) in 1953 to take the heavyweight championship. During the decade, Marciano bested five challengers to keep the title. He retired with a lifetime record of 49 victories and no losses, probably the best record of any prizefighter.

In sports, as in all areas of U.S. life in the 1950s, the cold war was always in the background. The Olympic Games were then seen by many as a competition between the United States and its allies and the Soviet Union and its allies.

The 1952 Winter Games were the first in which the Soviet Union took part. The Soviet government decided that its athletes would live outside of the Olympic Village, which housed the rest of the world's competitors. Yet relations between athletes from the communist and noncommunist countries were friendly.

It was a different story during the Summer Games in 1956, which were held in Melbourne, Australia, not long after the Soviet invasion of Hungary. In protest against the invasion, several countries refused to send athletes to the games. The United States chose to compete, but the Soviets won 99 medals as opposed to 74 for the United States.

The Soviets also earned more medals than the United States in the 1960 Summer Olympics, held in Rome, Italy. These games included several triumphs for African-American athletes. Wilma Rudolph, Rafer Johnson, and Lee Calhoun all performed brilliantly in the track-and-field events, and a young boxer named Cassius Clay took the gold medal in heavyweight boxing. A few years later, Clay would change his name to Muhammad Ali.

"We are not saints. We know we make mistakes, but our hearts are in the right place."

—President Eisenhower on U.S.-Latin American relations, 1960

THE ELECTION OF 1960

Despite the troubles of his second term, President Eisenhower remained popular as the decade ended. Despite his age, his health was better than it had been during the election of 1956. Eisenhower might have run for a third time, but in 1951 the Twenty-Second Amendment to the Constitution had become law. This amendment limited presidents to two four-year terms and was mainly a result of President Franklin Roosevelt's unprecedented four-term presidency.

The Republican nomination in 1960 went to the man who had served as vice president for eight years, Richard Nixon. Massachusetts senator Henry Cabot Lodge Jr. was his running mate. The Democratic

Richard Nixon speaks on the campaign trail in 1960. The Republican candidate hoped that his experience as Dwight Eisenhower's vice-president would give him the edge in the presidential election. *(Library of Congress)*

"The path of reason and common sense is open if the Soviets will but use it."

—President Eisenhower after the Paris summit of 1960

nominee was the other senator from Massachusetts, John F. Kennedy, with Senator Lyndon Johnson of Texas in the vice-presidential spot.

Nixon and Kennedy were alike in many ways. Both were young by the standards of most presidential candidates: Nixon was 47 years old in 1960, Kennedy was 43. Both were navy veterans of World War II. Despite their party differences, both were determined anticommunists.

Nixon, however, came from a modest Quaker background in California, while Kennedy grew up as part of a prominent Massachusetts family with a

John F. Kennedy won the presidency with just one-half of one percent of the popular vote more than Richard Nixon—the closest presidential election in American history until the 2000 contest between Al Gore and George W. Bush. *(Library of Congress)*

FASHIONS OF THE 1950S

Women's fashions of the 1950s were influenced by the New Look style that developed in France after World War II. New Look dresses hugged the figure and used lots of fabric in the skirt. They were often worn with shoes that featured the new spike-like stiletto heel. Men's business attire was dominated by two-piece, single-breasted suits in conservative colors such as black and gray.

Men usually wore hats when not at home or in the office; that is, until after the election of 1960. Because President Kennedy did not like to wear hats, many men followed his lead and went bareheaded. Teenagers of the 1950s had styles all their own, including poodle skirts with appliqué designs and saddle shoes for girls. Blue jeans and sneakers were popular with both sexes.

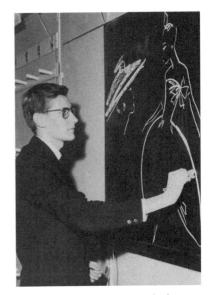

Yves St. Laurent succeeded Christian Dior in 1957 as head designer of France's leading fashion house. His designs— which lengthened skirts and incorporated beatnik elements like black turtleneck sweaters— were very influential in American women's fashions. *(Library of Congress)*

wealthy and politically powerful father. Kennedy was also a Roman Catholic. The United States had never had a Catholic president, and Kennedy's religion became an issue in the campaign—proof that religious as well as racial prejudice was still a part of U.S. society, even in the mid-20th century.

Nixon had more experience at the highest level of government, but Kennedy had great personal charm and was an inspiring speaker. In his speech accepting his party's nomination, Kennedy called on the nation to face the challenges of the decade ahead:

> *We stand at the edge of a New Frontier—the frontier of unfulfilled hopes and dreams. It will deal with unsolved problems of peace and war, unconquered pockets of ignorance and prejudice, unanswered questions of poverty and surplus.*

In October, the two candidates met for a series of televised debates. In his 1952 Checkers speech, Nixon had used the power of television to save his political career. In the 1960 presidential debates, however, that same power seemed to work against him. On-screen, Kennedy appeared confident and relaxed, while Nixon's perspiring face made him seem nervous and less able.

The original Barbie Doll sported accessories including sunglasses, sandals, and earrings. *(Library of Congress)*

THE BARBIE DOLL

In the 1950s, husband-and-wife business partners Elliot and Ruth Handler ran a growing toy company named Mattel. While watching her young daughter Barbara and her friends at play, Ruth Handler noticed that the girls had more fun dressing up adult paper dolls than they did playing with baby or child dolls. She decided to make a three-dimensional, plastic adult female doll that girls could dress up with different outfits and accessories. (Handler was also inspired by a German doll she had seen while on a trip to Europe.) Named Barbie after the Handlers' daughter, the 11 and a half inch doll made its debut at the 1959 New York Toy Fair. Many toy makers and store owners thought the new doll would fail, but when the first Barbies reached store shelves (priced at $3), they were an instant hit with young girls.

Over the next 10 years, Mattel sold more than $500 million worth of Barbie dolls, clothes, and other items. Not everyone loved Barbie, however. Critics pointed out that the doll bore little resemblance to real-life adult women. Others charged that the doll would make girls think that clothing, jewelry, and hairstyles were the most important concerns for adult women. Nevertheless, Barbie was here to stay. By the 21st century, two Barbie dolls were sold every second around the world.

Many people who listened to the debates on the radio felt that Nixon did a better job than Kennedy, but millions more who saw them on television believed that Kennedy was the clear winner in the debates. The election was one of the closest in U.S. history, but when all the votes were counted, Kennedy had won by about 120,000 popular votes.

THE LEGACY OF THE 1950S

The decade ahead would be one of the most challenging times in the nation's history. U.S. society would undergo huge changes in the 1960s. For this reason, many Americans would later look back on the 1950s as a decade of peace and calm before the storms of the 1960s.

The reality is more complicated. As historian David Halberstam points out in his book *The Fifties,* many of the trends of the 1960s really began in the 1950s. The civil rights movement, which would peak with Martin Luther King Jr.'s 1963 March on Washington, and the passage of the Civil Rights Act of 1964, and the Voting Rights Act of 1965, began with *Brown v. Board of Education,* the Montgomery bus boycott, and the Little Rock crisis of the 1950s. And the space race, which the United States finally won in 1969 by landing the first humans on the moon, started with the *Sputnik* launch and the U.S. response to the Soviet space challenge.

Similarly, the nation's involvement in Vietnam, which would turn into a major war in 1964, began with U.S. support for the French war in Indochina and with President Eisenhower's belief in the domino theory. And U.S. involvement in the Middle East can be traced back to events such as the Suez Crisis of 1956.

The Beat movement helped inspired the hippies of the 1960s and influenced many other social changes of that decade—from the debate about women's role in society to concerns over the power of the military-industrial complex.

For these reasons, the 1950s marked the beginning of changes in U.S. society that Americans are still dealing with today. The mid-century decade was a turning point in U.S. culture.

"We have beaten you to the moon, but you have beaten us in sausage making."

—Khrushchev, referring to the unmanned Soviet spacecraft that reached the moon in 1959, comments on the hot dog, in Des Moines, Iowa, in 1959

GLOSSARY

automation   Replacement of human labor by machines in industry.

blacklisting   Denying work to people because of their political beliefs.

censure   An official statement of disapproval.

census   The federal government's survey of the nation's population, carried out every 10 years.

civil rights   The right to vote, the right to a fair trial, the right to serve on juries, and other rights.

communism   A political system in which the government controls all property in the name of the people.

containment   The U.S. policy of preventing communist expansion after World War II.

coup   The violent overthrow of a nation's government by an opposition group, often by military officers.

demilitarized zone (DMZ)   The heavily guarded border between the nations of North and South Korea.

depression   A period of high unemployment accompanying an economic slowdown.

deterrence   A strategy by which a nation attempts to deter, or avoid, nuclear war by having a large supply of nuclear weapons.

dictator   A leader who rules with absolute power.

fad   An activity that enjoys a brief but widespread period of popularity.

federal deficit   The shortage that occurs when the federal government spends more than it collects.

inflation   A sharp rise in the prices of goods and services.

integration   The process of ending segregation by race.

labor union   A group of workers who join together to win better treatment and higher wages from employers.

midterm elections   Congressional elections held two years after every presidential election.

musical   A play that includes songs.

National Guard   Military units called up by each state that are under the control of the governor or the federal government.

nationalism   A movement dedicated to the independence and self-government of a nation.

nuclear family   A household made up only of two parents and their children.

pesticide   A chemical used to kill insects that spread disease or prey on crops.

price supports   Payments to farmers by the federal government to help them make a profit from the sale of their crops.

radiation   A form of energy released in a nuclear reaction that can be harmful to people and other living things.

recession   A period of higher than normal unemployment and decreased economic activity.

Secret Service   Agents of the U.S. Treasury who act as bodyguards for the president and other high-ranking government officials.

segregation   The system of separate facilities for whites and blacks in much of the South, which lasted from the 1890s to the 1960s.

space race   The competition between the United States and the Soviet Union to be the first to achieve milestones in space exploration.

State Department   The branch of the federal government that oversees diplomatic relations between the United States and other countries.

suburbs   Residential communities close to major cities.

truce   An agreement by both sides engaged in a war to stop fighting until final peace terms can be negotiated.

United Nations   The international organization set up after World War II to promote world peace and cooperation among nations.

urban renewal   The planned destruction and rebuilding of rundown inner-city areas.

vaccine   A substance made of a weakened, killed, or partial version of the organisms that cause a particular disease. A vaccine is used to build up a resistance to the disease in the body of a vaccinated person.

white supremacy   The idea that whites are superior to blacks and those of other races.

FURTHER READING

BOOKS

Anderson, Dale. *The Atom Bomb Project* Landmark Events in American History. New York: World Almanac Library, 2004.

Bayley, Stephen. *Harley Earl and the Dream Machine*. New York: Knopf, 1983.

Brady, James. *The Coldest War: A Memoir of Korea*. New York: Crown, 1990.

Brenner, Samuel. *Dwight D. Eisenhower.* Presidents and Their Decisions. San Diego: Greenhaven Press, 2002.

Colman, Penny. *Where the Action Was: Women War Correspondents in World War II*. New York: Crown Books for Young Readers, 2002.

Crowe, Chris. *Getting Away with Murder: The True Story of the Emmett Till Case*. New York: Dial Books, 2003.

Durrett, Deanne. *The 1950s*. American History Decade by Decade. Farmington Hills, Mich.: KidHaven Press, 2003.

Egendorf, Laura K., and Jesse G. Cunningham. *The McCarthy Hearings*. At Issue in History. San Diego: Greenhaven Press, 2002.

Egendorf, Laura. *Harry S. Truman*. Presidents and Their Decisions. Farmington Hills, Mich.: Greenhaven Press, 2001.

Epstein, Dan. *The 50's*. 20th Century Pop Culture. New York: Chelsea House, 2000.

Feinstein, Stephen. *The 1950s: From the Korean War to Elvis* Decades of the 20th Century. Berkeley Heights, N.J.: Enslow, 2000.

Granfield, Linda. *I Remember Korea: Veterans Tell Their Stories of the Korean War, 1950–53*. New York: Clarion, 2003.

Hakim, Joy. *All the People 1945–1999*. A History of US, vol. 10. New York: Oxford University Press, 2002.

Isserman, Maurice. *The Korean War, Updated Edition*. Edited by John Bowman. America at War. New York: Facts On File, 2003.

Kallen, Stuart A. *The 1950s*. Cultural History of the United States through the Decades. San Diego: Lucent Books, 1999.

———. *The Baby Boom*. Turning Points in World History. Farmington Hills, Mich.: Greenhaven Press, 2001.

Kuhn, Betsy. *Angels of Mercy: The Army Nurses of World War II*. New York: Atheneum, 1999.

Lindop, Edmund. *America in the 1950s*. Westport, Conn.: Twenty-First Century Books, 2002.

Marling, Karal Ann. *As Seen on TV: The Visual Culture of Everyday Life in the 1950s.* Cambridge, Mass.: Harvard University Press, 1996.

Maus, Derek, ed. *Living Through The Red Scare*. Farmington Hills, Mich.: Greenhaven Press, 2005.

May, Elaine Tyler. *Pushing the Limits: American Women 1940–1961*. Young Oxford History of Women in the United States. vol. 9. New York: Oxford University Press, 1994.

Morrison, Toni. *Remember: The Journey to School Integration*. Boston: Houghton Mifflin, 2004.

Nelson, Peter. *Left for Dead*. New York: Delacorte Books for Young Readers, 2003.

Panchyk, Richard. *World War II for Kids: A History with 21 Activities*. Chicago: Chicago Review Press, 2002.

Shapiro, Laura. *Something from the Oven: Reinventing Dinner in 1950s America*. New York: Viking, 2004.

Sherrow, Victoria. *Joseph McCarthy and the Cold War*. Notorious Americans and Their Times. Farmington Hills, Mich.: Blackbirch Press, 1998.

Steins, Richard. *The Postwar Years: the Cold War and the Atomic Age (1950-1959).* New York: 21st Century, 1997.

Time-Life Books. *The American Dream: The 50s.* Our American Century. New York: Time-Life Books, 2000.

Time-Life Books. *Rock & Roll Generation: Teen Life in the 50s.* Our American Century. New York: Time-Life Books, 1998.

Thomas, Joyce Carol. *Linda Brown, You Are Not Alone: The Brown v. Board of Education Decision.* New York: Jump at the Sun, 2003.

Turck, Mary. *The Civil Rights Movement for Kids: A History with 21 Activities.* Chicago: Chicago Review Press, 2000.

Warren, James. *Cold War: The American Crusade against the Soviet Union and World Communism, 1945–1990.* New York: HarperCollins, 1996.

Wilson, Camilla. *Rosa Parks: From the Back of the Bus to the Front of a Movement.* New York: Scholastic, 2001.

World War II. DK Eyewitness Books. New York: DK Publishing, 2004.

Yenne, Bill. *Going Home to the Fifties.* San Francisco: Last Gasp, 2002.

Young, Nancy K., and William H. Young. *The 1950s.* American Popular Culture Through History. Westport, Conn.: Greenwood Press, 2004.

Zeinert, Karen. *McCarthy and the Fear of Communism in American History.* Berkeley Heights, N.J.: Enslow, 1998.

WEBSITES

"Fifties Web," Available online. URL: www. fiftiesweb.com/fifties.htm. Downloaded on June 16, 2005.

Library of Congress American Memory. "Rosa Parks," Available online. URL: http://lcweb2. loc.gov/ammem/today/ dec01.html. Downloaded on June 16, 2005.

Linder, Douglas, University of Missouri, Kansas City. "The Rosenberg Trial." Available online. URL: http://www.law.umkc.edu/ faculty/projects/ ftrials/rosenb/ROSENB.HTM. Updated in 2001.

Long Island Universtity. "Martin Luther King, Jr." Available online. URL: http://www.liu.edu/ cwis/cwp/library/mlking.htm. Downloaded on June 16, 2005.

National Civil Rights Museum. "Civil Rights." Available online. URL: http://www. civilrightsmuseum.org/. Downloaded on June 16, 2005.

Television History. "1950–1959," Available online. URL: http://www.tvhistory.tv/1950-1959.htm. Downloaded on June 16, 2005.

The History Channel. Available online. URL: http://www.historychannel.com/exhibits/ fifties/. Downloaded on June 16, 2005.

U.S. Army. "Korean War," Available online. URL: http://korea50.army.mil/. Updated on September 30, 2003.

Weingrof, Richard, U.S. Department of Transportation, Federal Highway Division. "The Interstate Highway System," Available online. URL: http://www.tfhrc.gov/pubrds/ summer96/p96su10.htm. Downloaded on June 16, 2005.

White House. "Harry Truman, "Available online. URL: http://www.whitehouse.gov/ history/ presidents/ht33.html. Downloaded on June 16, 2005.

White House. "Dwight Eisenhower," Available online. URL: http://www.whitehouse.gov/ history/presidents/de34.html. Downloaded on June 16, 2005.

INDEX

Page numbers in *italics* indicate illustrations. Page numbers followed by *g* indicate glossary entries. Page numbers in **boldface** indicate box features.